# GOD'S FAVORITE 21ST CENTURY ANGEL

## DEVIN K. PARRISH

Strategic Book Publishing
New York, New York

Strategic Book Publishing
An imprint of Writers Literary & Publishing Services, Inc.
845 Third Avenue, 6th Floor – 6016
New York, NY 10022

http://www.strategicbookpublishing.com

ISBN: 978-1-60860-548-4

Printed in the United States of America

# ACKNOWLEDGEMENTS

Thank you: God for the gifts, Jesus for the example and Holy Spirit for the guidance; Dad, I am completely free in your love. Thank you for being a fearless father to a child like me; Edna, thanks for being a patient wife to my father and a great friend to me; Bonnie, you're one of my biggest cheerleaders! Thank you for your tears, laughter, encouragement and for listening to my endless stories about my parents; D'—you wrote the letter that ignited the flame! Heather, Kyna, Narinder and Ms. Aida thanks for always asking, "How's the book coming?" at just the right time; Don and Julie—the drive to Lawrenceville is always worth it!; Uncle Bill and Aunt Supat for your availability and timely wisdom; Randy (I love you extra-something!), Kenny, Kathy and the rest of my family and friends, most of whom were unaware I was writing this book, and the countless mix CDs that inspired me to dance and sing through this!

# CONTENTS

# BEGINNINGS

By Gladine Parrish

I was very angry growing up in the Jim Crow days, standing to be served, being called "nigger," "gal," or anything that was permissible.

I had to go in the back door of the house of the white family for whom my mom made me do manual labor. The one salary I can remember was $1.50 a week. I was only ten years old and I washed the family's clothes, hung them out and took them down, starched them with cooked starch, sprinkled them, ironed them, washed the porch, which stretched around the entire house, washed windows, cleaned blinds in the bathtub, moved furniture to clean under and behind them, waxed and buffed wood floors, and vacuumed carpets. Here's the clincher: I had to go home to eat lunch and come back to this slave camp!

I was eleven when the oldest son got married to the community doctor's daughter and I had to fix the pretty food for the second reception that was given. I was able to do all these things because my mom was the greatest cook on earth and she thought all of her girls would grow up to marry a great man and we needed to know all of these things.

By the time I turned twelve, I had been chosen to play first base for an all boys softball team and was excelling in basketball. I waited until this mean person I was slaving for called me names and was giving me many orders early in the day to tell her I was quitting. She started to hit me and I stood still and told her that if she hit me, I would kick her white butt. She wasn't sure I would follow through because I was smaller than she, but she could see I wasn't afraid of her, so she backed off and begged me not to leave, but I just turned and walked away.

My mom didn't like that at all, but I was not made to go back. I wouldn't have even if I had been told to. I would've just taken my punishment. I had already had more whippings in the family than anyone else, so what was another one going to do?

Except for the racism and mysterious killings of black men, and many things going on as I grew up with nine sisters and brothers, I had a great time growing up in the mountains of Chattaroy, West Virginia where I lived until I was an adult.

My mom shipped us off to either school or a job as soon as we graduated from high school. She decided that I would go to nursing school since the older siblings had been fortunate enough to go to college directly from high school, and that stopped at me. What I didn't know at first was that the nursing school was psychiatric nursing inside a mental hospital.

There were two women who were patients there, Clara and Liz. They had been locked in seclusion for more than thirty years and most of the nurses were afraid to go in their room and give them water and food. One evening I was working the floor alone and decided they had gone long enough without those things even though they were completely insane. I gathered trays and took my keys, opened the door, and went in. When I turned my back to them to sit the tray down, I felt an iron rail against my head. It became the two of them against me. I was very strong, but not that strong. They finally beat me unconscious. I don't know how long I was out before someone found me, lying there, bleeding.

I spent two months in the hospital getting blood transfusions and being treated for a skull fracture, broken shoulder, and broken pelvis.

But Clara and Liz had tuberculosis, and I caught it from them. As a result, I spent one year flat on my back in a sanitarium in another part of the mountains to be sure no one caught it.

TB was fatal in those days and I had to wait at home for a room because the beds in the sanitarium were all filled. Basically, I was waiting for someone to die.

I was so healthy and strong that I walked around for a long time before the tuberculosis was discovered.

The mental hospital's softball team had gotten our new spiked shoes and was practicing sliding in them. When I hit the ball and ran to first base, I slid and was out cold. The TB was very advanced. Before that, I spent endless hours coughing and having night sweats, but everyone just thought I had a bad cold.

I was put in the clinic and my parents were called to come get me. My mom came and my oldest brother drove her. The drive from where we lived was several hours. Despite my severe illness, Mom decided that instead of TB, I was sick because I had become pregnant and tried to get rid of the baby. I was shocked because, at eighteen, I was still a virgin, but Mom never believed that.

By the time I got home, I was hemorrhaging from my mouth and nose. I had gotten so skinny in a matter of weeks. I eventually lost all my strength and could no longer even hold a glass of water.

The saintly women in the community who helped raise me and love me developed shifts and each one took turns staying with me around the clock and kept their routine until there was a bed for me at the sanitarium.

They had to hold me up and hold my head to put water in my mouth. By then, I wasn't eating anything and sometimes they would pour clear broth or soup in my mouth and it was always impossible to swallow because my throat had nearly closed up. I was less than one hundred pounds.

My entrance exam determined that I would be dead in less than a month. I was in that sanitarium for two years, but I walked out of there. That was more than forty-eight years ago and by the grace of God I am still here and the doctor who predicted I would die died more than forty years ago.

When I was a child, I attended a two-room school for blacks only until I reached seventh grade. At that time, I started catching a bus at 6:45 A.M. and rode all across the hills and mountains, picking up kids nestled within them. We always got the old buses that the white schools didn't use anymore.

One of our drivers was a war veteran who'd lost his leg and wore a poorly-fitted wooden leg. I always thought that's why he smelled of alcohol, but I adored him. I could tell from his shaggy beard and red eyes that, at some point in his life, this man was a hunk. At my forty-ninth school reunion, I met a lady who said she was his daughter and she had heard her father speak of me often.

In my eighth grade year, our first high school band was formed. I was chosen as the first drum majorette, but shortly after we got started, I was stricken with Rheumatic Fever.

We had been playing hide and seek in our backyard when all of a sudden my legs and chest became very tired and my arms felt heavy. Parents started calling their kids home when it got dark. Everybody went home and my siblings went inside the house. When I started to get up, my legs, arms, and everything from the waist down were frozen. I was paralyzed. My dad kept coming to the back door, yelling for me to get inside and go to bed. I told him that I couldn't move and he thought I was pretending so I could stay outside longer (In the dark by myself? Get real, Dad!). When he decided there really was something wrong with me, he came to where I was sitting, picked me up, and carried me into the house. I didn't feel a thing.

The community doctor took care of everyone, including Howard Holler, Black Bottom (no, it wasn't named for black people), Buffalo, Up-the-Holler, and Down-the-Holler.

This doctor was very wealthy and very loving and smart. He used the same glass for everybody who needed to take a pill while in his office. He didn't make a difference with race.

The glass was never washed, only rinsed out with cold water between users. That famous glass was pretty clear in the beginning, but the last time I used it, it was a deep, rusty brown.

He made hospital calls for the white people and house calls for the Negroes.

My mother never let me forget that I weighed fourteen pounds at birth and the doctor received an award from the American Medical Association for delivering me.

The reason it was such a difficult birth was because I was a breech baby—my arm and leg were coming out first. The doctor left it up to my dad as to whom he should save, me or Mom. He said, "Save my wife. I can do without another baby."

He was soon to learn that he could not do without me. Even until his death, I teased him about how on earth he could have made it if he had gotten rid of me.

My mom had a baby that weighed almost twenty pounds and the doctor could not save him. He was a beautiful baby; my dad took pictures of him in his casket. The doctor had to crush his skull so he could get him out of my mom without killing her.

She had eight more babies after me.

After my bout with Rheumatic Fever, I went back to school, but my spot in front of the band was replaced by a girl I've known all my life.

Our band was the smallest in the state, but the greatest and the baddest. We had a bandmaster who wasn't much older than we were and almost every girl had a crush on him.

My dad launched a drive to buy our instruments, which were paid for with cash. He then raised money to buy uniforms. My head was so big that I had to have a special hat made and it was retired after I graduated. They never let me forget that! I'm still teased when we have our school reunions. We have school reunions, not class reunions, because we only had between two hundred and three hundred students in the entire school, sometimes less.

We competed in every statewide band competition for blacks only. We always won first place for maneuvering, performing, and a few times for instrumentalists. I ended up playing clarinet sometimes, mostly by ear, bell lyre by ear, and bass drums. I would use three drumsticks and I kept one in the air when we marched, using the other two to hit the drums. I used to burst with pride, especially when I could hear my dad bragging about me and pointing me out as we marched through town before a home or away game.

Our basketball teams won state championships almost every year. My oldest brother was a star when he played basketball and football, and my second brother was even better.

We who lived out in the sticks were better players because our parents always cut a hole in a bushel basket and nailed it to a tree and we played all the time.

We had no inside water and most of the women washed in tin tubs with the boards. My dad thought he was a big shot, so naturally we had a Maytag washer, which my mom said was the best ever.

Mom always washed on Mondays, no matter what was going on, and she did for as long as she was able, up until her early 80s. We had to carry water in buckets from across the railroad tracks where the closest water pump was located.

We had to straighten every room, including making beds, get up early enough to cook Dad's breakfast before he left for the coal mines up in the hills at 4:30 A.M., separate the clothes, wash dishes, fix sack lunches, sometimes even pick whatever fruit and vegetables were ripe in the garden, which was in our very big yard and on the hill. We also had to get soiled diapers ready for the wash, and I know I am missing something.

We took turns doing homework while the others did chores. Mom had three irons and three ironing boards, real ones, but I never knew about the irons I hear people talking about that you stick in the fire or whatever. Like I said, we were so-called "big shots."

We had to make a fire under the big black tub sitting on bricks in the backyard and fill the washer with hot water and two rinse tubs that sat on the back porch, even in the winter. Carrying water was a continuous thing until we had enough for Mom to change washer water two or three times. I thought she was totally crazy back then.

She made the lye soap, she cooked the starch perfectly, and in the white clothes she added bluing; I think that was something that was supposed to make the clothes very bright.

She sewed all of our clothes except the ones she bought in Alden, Montgomery Ward, and Sears catalogues. We all owned leather jackets, even in those days. We all had sport shoes, shorts, school shoes, dress shoes, school boots, coats, jackets, and dress boots.

We raised chickens that laid eggs. We killed them and took the feathers off so Mom could cook them. We raised every vegetable and fruit that was heard of. We bought very little from the company store that sold everything a family needed. The men would get unlimited credit in that store.

Even then, my mom loved to spend money and shop, and she did so with my dad's blessings. He truly loved my mom and did not let her work until all of us were in school. It didn't keep him from having other women but he kept it away from Mom, so he thought. I am sure she knew, because I knew.

We would plow the dirt in our yard and on the hill. I can remember the plow that was too wide for my arms to reach and hold comfortably. So, I had to stretch and skip to keep up with the horse pulling the plow. We all had our turn.

My dad had two sheds built in our yard, one to store kindling (firewood) for the winter, which was chopped by the boys every year before winter. Dad would order a truckload of the wood and we had three axes and three saws and I still have a scar on my knee right now to prove we had sharp saws.

The other shed was for us to play house in. That was a big favorite in the neighborhood. I wasn't one to play Mom and Dad. Yes, that was going on in my day. I remember an older girl who was out of high school being the mother and one of my classmates was the father and they were always trying to make babies all the time—I mean for real! It made me angry that she infringed on our playtime in order for her to introduce the boys our ages to sex.

Mom cooked breakfasts like biscuits, chicken, pork chops, steaks, fried apples, eggs, grits, oatmeal, fried potatoes, hot rolls –things that I haven't been able to afford hardly since I reached adulthood.

Each Thanksgiving, all the friends in the neighborhood got together to slaughter hogs. We had one man who did all the shooting and he had a command that only the hogs understood. He was the man who built, added on to rooms, or whatever the women of the community wanted. He was certainly a jack-of-all-trades.

We all had to help with the hogs. I was one of the ones who had to clean the guts known as chitterlings. I had to squeeze the stuff out of the skin into the creek and turn the gut inside out and rinse them clean in the clear creek. I can't believe I ended up really liking chitterlings, even to this day, but can no longer eat them because I am an old woman with all kinds of health negatives.

The men would cut the head off the hog and cut it into hams, pork chops, sausages, tenderloins, and many things that we pay a fortune for now. The women would prepare the meat for winter storage. They made gauze bags for the sausage after seasoning them, like you never had before in your life! They cooked the waste fat and skin and made tons of lard. They would save the brains and cook them with scrambled eggs. They would cook the head and something else I can no longer remember, and make this great souse meat and form it into loaves for mostly sandwiches. I am craving this as I write.

They saved the tails, feet; every part of the hog was edible. My dad built a smoke house in the yard next to the chicken house and hooks to hang the hams, shoulders, and bacon.

My mom would can the fresh vegetables, the fruit from the trees and vines that we owned. I think we raised every kind of fruit except bananas and pineapples. She even made bread loaves and rolls, white and wheat. She made all kinds of candy the year sugar was rationed due to one of the wars.

We had a youth center in town that did not sell liquor, but had food, drinks, and lots of dancing. We were really a dancing bunch of kids. We all thought we were the greatest. I still love to dance, but I am hampered by crippling arthritis.

We also had buses that ran until eleven or twelve at night. That was a blessing because only a couple of the adults had a car and it was not us. But everyone shared their cars for the needs of the entire community.

We were supposed to sit in the back of the bus, but the bus drivers all knew my father and they knew he had one daughter who was not going to sit in the back and neither were her sisters who traveled with her!

My two younger sisters would always want to go to town with me, especially when I was playing for a church in town. We would visit the bookstore and stock up on candy and funny books. One would always sit with me and the other had to sit with someone. When a white passenger saw that one of us had to sit with them, they would put their hand on the empty part of the seat. My sisters were so chicken and they would always tell me, "Her hand is on the seat," and I would tell them to sit on their hand. That would make the person move their hand or even get up and give us the entire seat, which was fine with me.

I was so angry that we had to go through all of the mess and we were just kids who were trying to grow up and have clean fun, but it was almost impossible. We faced things everyday, especially me because my reputation preceded me. Even white adults would pick on me, especially if I was by myself. I almost got into trouble many times. They hated that when they stomped their foot and called me "nigger" I wouldn't even flinch. If they tried to put their hands on me, I would threaten them with the fear of my big 6'4" black dad and most of the time, it would make them back off.

They plotted to kill my dad but he also showed no fear of them. I was really a chip off the old black block. I wasn't tall or big yet, but I was tough and loved to fight and would at the blink of an eye.

My parents taught me to love, and not hate, but if it had been up to me, I am sure I would have hated many people, especially the ones who hindered my growth and the ability to act on the talents with which I was so richly blessed.

We had great teachers in our two-room school with big burnside heaters and wooden, oiled floors and lots of windows. My mom, wanting to make extra money, was the janitor at our school, but of course, we were the workers and she was the supervisor and the treasurer. As small as I was, even going to town to school, I had to lift those industrial mops and big push brooms and lift buckets of oil that we poured on the dirty wooden floors to give them a clean look. I had never heard of that method before, nor have I heard of it since.

We had outdoor toilets, one for boys and one for girls. Ours had two seats inside to sit on and do what we had to do. It was also like a clubhouse where some of us inquisitive girls met and listened to the one experienced girl tell us about things that we had never heard of before in our lives. She was the one who told me about menstruation and showed us herself when she was on her period, changing the rags that she wore, since none of us had ever heard of sanitary pads either.

I didn't think much about all of that because I thought I was so far away from it. Our mom never told us a thing about sex, periods, or anything. She always warned us about letting boys get up under our clothes. That was it. I always tried to imagine what it would be like for a boy to get under my clothes. I just thought that a boy would crawl or just get on the floor and really get under our clothes! I found no excitement or danger in the thought of that.

I didn't even start having my period until I was seventeen and out of high school. I didn't connect it to getting married or having children.

Most of the girls had very long, thick hair and long legs, clear complexions; we were very pretty girls but didn't know it then. The first time anyone told me I was pretty was when I went to town to school in the seventh grade. A very shy boy told me I was very pretty.

I hated my long, thick, heavy hair because it got in the way of my sports activities. I had a hard time finding a means to keep it up or back out of my way.

I never thought about disobeying my parents. I thought listening and obeying without question was a part of growing up. Now, I always had questions and objections and I was whipped a lot for being so outspoken. When my mom had the nerve to tell me I couldn't got to a basketball game with no real reason except she was the adult and I was the child, I would object until she had to beat me down to the ground. I would keep ranting and raving and she would give up beating me because I was so small and bony and a lot of times she would break a finger or leave lasting scars on my body that I would show to anyone who would take time to look. I would tell people that she was my stepmother and hated me.

I would always run and she would send my brother after me and I would kick his butt and he would give up in defeat. There was no way that I was going to stand still and be beaten. My mom had to really work hard to whip me, but she always did. I always wondered why we got so many whippings. We never got in trouble with the law, we were in everything and excelled in them, we made good grades, and we did all the work around the house. I got many whippings by telling her that it was her job to do all that stuff, and it would be my job to do it in my house after I finished growing up and got married and had my own house. But it only gave her more excuses to keep hitting me.

Many times I thought about hitting her back or picking up a brick and knocking her out cold with it. When I locked myself in the outside toilet one time, she forced her hands through the crack in the door and was pulling on the door, making the lock break loose. I looked down on the floor and saw a big rock. I picked it up and held it, trying to decide to come down on her fingers with it and just give up living totally. She always said if she even thought I was thinking about hitting her, she would kill me. Now, would she really have killed me? Oh, how I wanted to call her bluff.

It was adventurous to me to hear her and Dad talk about killing us and Dad would say if we did certain things, he would take his shotgun and blow our heads off. If we were criminal kids, it would have made a little sense, but we didn't even raise our voices when we talked to them.

I was whipped for rolling my eyes in disgust, sighing heavily, or taking one and a half seconds to move when she told me to do something.

I would bleed from those beatings, and if my basketball fingers or drum hands or piano hands would get broken, Mom would make a batter with corn meal and something very stinky and make a splint and spread the smelly stuff on my broken bones and wrap it with clean strips of cloths. I would take it off as soon as I got out of sight and show the disfiguration to all my friends and teachers. They thought Mom was very mean, but they didn't know I drove her crazy.

After we were adults and had children of our own, I used to tease them when they were too old and tired to do anything. I told both of them if we had the laws that we have now, back then, they would both still be serving their time in prison for the beatings they gave me.

Our community had things to interest the children as well as the adults. Each year, there was a beauty contest and the same girls were up to compete against each other, mostly for the satisfaction of our mothers.

We had terrific ball games in the white schoolyard. This included our parents and everyone in the neighborhood. The black churches fellowshipped together, too.

We had a picnic that included all the black churches, even the ones over, through, and across the mountains. It was colossal. You have never tasted homemade ice cream, cakes, pies, cobblers, and watermelon; the watermelons in the stores now aren't even related to the ones we had growing up.

We had relay races, broad jump contests, and we won real prizes, nothing expensive, just something enough to encourage the talents in the different children.

No one was ashamed to own Jesus in those days. Even we kids would talk about our relationship with God when we were just sitting around talking. We had the best Bible schools in the summer. We only had professional people in charge. We had classes according to our age groups and Bible scriptures that we were required to learn are still in our hearts and minds some fifty or sixty years later. One of the most important things we had to memorize was all the names of the books of the Bible, Old and New Testaments. I still know them.

We had 4-H Club, which had a strong influence on our culture and intelligence. Our dads used to take rakes and shovels and clean out the bottom of the creek, taking out the glass, sticks, rocks, and rubbish, and they would stop the creek with planks and tie a rope on a strong tree branch. This was our swimming pool. We were not allowed in the beautiful pool at the community club for whites only. But it didn't stop us from being some of the greatest swimmers and divers to come from that part of the country. I loved swimming and we had so much fun.

The rope on the branch was our trapeze to swing out as far as we had nerves to, and let go and just fall in the water. We would stand on a strong branch far up from the pool and balance ourselves and do corrective diving.

There was a 4-H Camp several miles from where we lived and each year, right at school closing, we would fill up a Greyhound bus and travel to the camp. I will never forget the size of the pool and the great trails and animals. We learned to utilize the crops and animals we had on our farmland at home.

We also had junior conventions with the churches throughout the summer and fall. It taught us how to transact business like God would want us to. Each year, when it was held in a nearby city, each church would select a delegate or two and pay their way to observe and take notes during a two- or three-day session and bring a report back to our home churches.

If any girl from our hometown didn't know how to make things like sewing clothes, making home made ice cream and from scratch cakes, pies, or rolls, something was wrong.

In those days, that was the first requirement when a guy chose a girl, unless he was just plain crazy. Every guy in those days loved to eat good home-cooked food and a girl who could cook from scratch was very popular with the guys. There were no boxed cakes or frozen food in the stores because most people didn't have refrigerators and those who did, there was only space for a couple of ice trays, I think. I can't remember ice trays when I was a child, but I do know we never had an icebox in my day.

# GRIEF

The memories come in waves. Sometimes they're several low tides, linear but out of order: an eleven-year-old me squealing when Mom walks in from the grocery store, surprising me with the latest ELLE magazine; a six-year-old me sitting on three throw pillows between Mom's smooth, Vaselined legs getting my hair brushed and combed, a cup of water and a bottle of lotion on the floor next to her right foot, the sound of her large hands rummaging through the plastic bag where the ribbons she put in my hair were tangled into a huge ball; a five-year-old me, looking down at Mom, laughing, as she lies on the floor, bench pressing and tickling me.

Then tears fill my lower lids and fall. Sound doesn't always accompany them. My eyes just look straight ahead, glazed over, trying to see if I can store every detail of those memories in a special place in my brain. ELLE, ribbons, flight. ELLE, ribbons, flight. ELLE, ribbons, flight. ELLE, ribbons, flight. I can't forget the details: her fingers, her eyes, her nose, her scent.

Sometimes the memories are tidal waves, gigantic and inde-structible. They come while I'm driving, making the road a blur, or while I'm looking at the sky, imagining her somewhere beyond it: the smell of her turkey and dressing; the first Thanks-giving without her, I couldn't get rid of the smell. It was like a scoop of it was hidden everywhere I went and I spent a week trying to find it; my post-work conversations with her, how I would talk to her during the drive home: "Mom, you wouldn't believe ..." She would always delay her errands so she wouldn't miss my call. Denying the reflex of dialing her phone number is unbearable sometimes.

The memory of her availability consumes me. She answered the phone practically every time I called. When I made the drive from Atlanta to Cincinnati to visit her, she always left her apartment door cracked open so I wouldn't have to fiddle with a key.

"I can't believe you didn't get a ticket, Devin. That was too quick," she would always say when I walked in. She'd usually be sitting, waiting for me to collapse in her arms. The TV would be on, distracting her from worrying about my safe arrival. The scent of a fresh Glade plug-in would kick up when my head hit the back of the couch.

Mom's death is not the worst part. There really is no one worst part. There are many, like being terrorized by all the mem-ories, especially when they come with sounds, scents, and lights, feeling like those memories are past tense and the only way I can keep them present is to repeat them to myself because they've made me who I am and influence who I'm going to be.

The worst part is having so many new things to say and experience and I have to deny the reflex of dialing her phone number.

# DAD

My father is beautiful.

When he's with you, he makes you feel like you're the only person who matters and that all your concerns and ideas are the only things he needs to listen to.

When Dad is present, I feel like even if I trip and fall flat on my face, it won't matter how other people laugh at me because Dad will still think I'm divine.

I understand why my mother fell in love with him: he's not afraid to be emotional, whether it's an appropriate display of anger, a hard laugh, or a heavy-hearted cry. He also gives you the confidence to do and be absolutely anything. I don't think anyone had ever made Mom feel that about herself. Before Dad, she was always the one telling others what they could accomplish.

Dad walked into Mom's life on a Sunday afternoon.

He and his college roommate were visiting Dad's childhood church during Thanksgiving Break from the University of

Missouri-Columbia. The church had just hired Mom to be its musical director. Dad saw her statuesque build and fiery afro perched on a platform in front of a piano, and immediately wanted to know who she was.

Dad hadn't had much experience with women before Mom. He didn't have many girlfriends in his past and was still a virgin. He may have felt inadequate in her presence, but that didn't stop him from uttering his first words to her after service—a silly question about her coat that was indicative of his youth and inexperience: "Is that leather or pleather?" to which Mom replied, "What?"

Months after leaving that forgettable impression on Mom, Dad was back in Glendale. His tuition money had run out and he hitchhiked his way back to Ohio from Missouri. He did the same thing to get to Mom's choir rehearsals until Mom saw him on the side of the road one day and started giving him rides to the church. It was during those rides and rehearsals that their bond over music began. But Dad was already in love. When he'd catch a ride with her, he'd memorize the scent of the Jean Nate perfume Mom was wearing and fantasize about sweeping her off her feet.

Mom was unhappily married at the time, but was still trying to honor her wedding vows and keep her children in a two-parent household. Dad slowly broke her resistance with each visit he made to the house she shared with her first husband, hanging out with Mom's two sons and daughter who weren't that far behind him in age. He grew to love Mom's children as if they were his own, but as his attachment to Mom and her kids intensified, it became harder for him to keep his love for her a secret.

There was a coffee table in Mom's living room, which they would lay on opposite sides of on the floor. Dad says he and Mom would look at each other through the legs of the table and mouth "I love you." Despite their making such a declaration, Dad didn't think Mom fell in love with him until much later. A huge part of her would not allow herself to fully explore such feelings for another man while still being married.

Dad's persistence eventually broke Mom down and I was born within adultery and out of wedlock. Mom was forty-three years old. Dad was twenty. Their love was original. They had no predecessors in their midst who'd loved like they did. They were all alone with their mutual God-given gift: a bottomless capacity to love.

It had to be a gift because they didn't have any examples of how to love from their own families. For the first time in either of their lives, they found another person with whom they could exercise that ability and around whom they could feel comfortable in their own lovability.

Dad calls us the trinity: the mother, the father, and the daughter wrapped in swaddling clothes. My parents were homeless when I was born and for a short while they lived with one of Mom's friends. When they were there, Dad would stay awake during the night to keep roaches off my body.

A good portion of my early years were mostly spent with Dad. He effortlessly braided my hair, fixed my lunch, and took me to school. For a couple years, Mom's was the main income while Dad attended art school and some days, I'd go with him to his classes. We'd go to the park, the museum, and the zoo. They were cheap or free activities we could enjoy together.

From Dad I've learned that time is one of the best ingredients for building a relationship. I don't always remember the specifics of the things he and I did, but I always remember the time we've spent and the new insights I gain from our conversations.

My turbulent freshman year in college signaled the collapse of our trinity. A relationship that began in adultery ended in adultery. My father went his separate way and I watched Mom almost die over his departure.

I love my father so much, but no one has ever made me angrier. I was especially furious with him while he and Mom broke up. I took Mom's side and, at the time, I thought that meant I had to villainize him.

He hadn't completely moved out during this time and he treated our home like a hotel. He would make brief appearances to shower and change clothes; mutter a fragmented sentence or two off to Mom and me, then disappear into the night and into a new life.

Dad would have these moments where he wouldn't talk to me at all. We went from spending hours talking about everything, to a few long, tension-filled silences and it really tore me up. I ran away to my Uncle Bill and Aunt Supat's in Michigan's Upper Peninsula and hid for about six months. They gave me my own little nook there, far away from my parents' demise.

Dad wrote me a lot while I was there, sometimes really long letters, most of which I kept. He'd write things like "I'm really glad you're getting this break, Devin" and "I'm glad things worked out the way they did, with you leaving and my not getting to see you off... .I still have a problem with tears."

Mom served as the peacemaker during mine and Dad's weird spastic tension, which lasted about six years. I stayed angry with Dad, not for leaving but for leaving in such a sloppy way. Mom was aware of my disgust, but didn't want me to stop loving him. I never stopped loving Dad; I just didn't like him at all anymore, especially when he would go through these phases of not speaking to me. I would wonder, "Why are you upset with me? You didn't cheat on me, you cheated on Mom!"

He was really shaken up about not being reachable when I'd gone to the hospital for my panic attack. The next afternoon, he and his wife came by Mom's to check up on me and he apologized. He looked at me with the same desperation in his eyes he had when I choked on a peppermint when I was nine.

The candy had lodged in my throat one Sunday afternoon when we were at Grandma and Granddad's. There was nothing anyone could do to move it, so Dad drove to the hospital in what felt like seconds. En route, he would blink a glance at the road, then stare at me in the rear view mirror. My initial fright subsided each time our eyes met, making my swallows a little less difficult.

My head took turns resting on Mom, Dad, and Grandma as we waited in the emergency room. Then, I felt the peppermint drop to my stomach. After not speaking for hours, I screamed, "It's gone!" Moments later, Dad cheered with me after a doctor confirmed that my saliva shrunk the candy enough to dislodge it.

After I returned from my final semester in college, Dad had stopped talking to me again, but it wasn't a disownership kind of silent treatment. He was immersed in a new life he was still trying to figure out and I don't think he'd figured out how to fit me in it yet. When we did talk, we disagreed on many things. In particular, I couldn't stand the church he was attending at the time and likened it to a cult. I also demanded that I not talk to him unless I could tell him exactly how I felt, but you can't have those kinds of conversations if the other person isn't ready. Despite all the braggadocio I was carrying around at the time, I wasn't ready for those kinds of conversations, either.

During one of mine and Dad's silent times, I was voicing my disgust to Mom and accidentally called her Dad. She said, "See? You two really need to talk. This is ridiculous."

A real resolution didn't come until Dad moved to Georgia about six months after I moved to Atlanta.

I got really upset with him when he told me he was moving. My fear was that he would start showing up unannounced in an effort to spend a bunch of catch-up time with me. I didn't even actually see him until he'd been in Georgia for a few months. It was my way of punishing him for doing something I didn't want him to do, not realizing his move was something that needed to be done.

Mom took turns scolding us for the vapidity of what our relationship had become. A turning point came when I'd abruptly ended a conversation with Dad. He called Mom and vented his frustration to her. She simply told him, "You're her father."

I eventually drove forty-five minutes to his new home and spent the weekend with him. It was the first time I'd seen him in almost a year. He was more beautiful than I remembered. Mom was eight hours away from our reunion. She probably had a huge grin on her face like she was in a corner of Dad's house watching us be together. The fractured, but still intact trinity was trying out this new awkward fit in different spaces.

# MUSIC

My earliest memories include the sounds Mom made on the piano. She was a church musician from the time her feet couldn't touch the pedals until her death. My feet didn't even hang over the front of the pew when I had my first visions of Mom teaching choir after choir three and four part harmonies. She was single-handedly responsible for these choral recitals that became outright productions. She handpicked soloists and constructed instrumental interludes with fellow musicians. These two sometimes-three-hour concerts became legendary. They made you believe music could bring everyone together.

Mom's posture at the piano was different from any pianist I'd ever seen. She would start off straight-backed and proper-fingered, then the Holy Spirit would take over and she'd hunch over, close her eyes, and some of her fingers would be stiff and straight, while the rest bent as if they were having spasms. Her hands pounded the keys with a thunderous weight. She would suck in her cheeks as the experience became more intense. If the singers were really at their best, she would stop playing and

25

just keep the beat on the pedals with her right foot. When the song ended, she opened her eyes in amnesic surprise. Afterward, when people would point out certain notes she'd hit, she often wouldn't even remember.

When we lived in Ft. Wayne, Indiana, there was a man who went to our church named Mr. Green who played an alto saxophone. He and Mom would do these amazing duets on some Sundays. Sometimes they would be jazzy improvisations, other times they'd be traditional hymns. Mom always allowed Mr. Green to shine. Her piano playing would merely be the pallet upon which Mr. Green could roll all over. They spoke to each other with their instruments, using a secret language only they could understand and that would only be spoken from the time they started to the time they stopped. Her chords would encourage him to keep making a joyful noise.

It always seemed like the sun would pierce through the church windows when they played. The rays were their spotlight spilling over onto their fingers, and when it was over, it was as if God abruptly turned the sun in another direction.

When I was four, we lived in a one-room apartment over a barbershop in Lockland, Ohio. We only had a sleeper sofa, a chair that a black and white TV sat on, and Dad's drafting table. I was so happy there, I don't even remember the windows icing over from the inside during the winter, which my parents said happened. I do remember sleeping in my underwear during the summer, sandwiched between my parents on the sofa bed near a fan that blew hot air. Their bodies were like two guardrails that kept all the monsters and boogie men far, far away. Our most prized possession was our record player. Mom, Dad, and I would sit for hours in front of it listening to album after album: Kenny Loggins, Walter and Tramaine Hawkins, Minnie Ripperton, Rufus featuring Chaka Khan, Chuck Mangione, Lakeside, Grover Washington, Jr., Stevie Wonder, the

Doobie Brothers, Vanessa Bell Armstrong, Fleetwood Mac.... It was a crash course in practically every musical genre and I was benefiting from this education before I even started kindergarten. During that same time, Mom was playing for a small church in Lockland. She was also the founder of a gospel sextet called God's Way of which my father was the only male member. He, along with Mom's friend Lena, held the tenor section, Rita and Denise were sopranos, and Annelle and Anna were altos. They rehearsed at Grandma and Granddad's house on Saturdays and had engagements in the Tri-State area. They were known for their flawless harmonies that I watched Mom drill them on until they could execute them without thinking.

Sitting in on those rehearsals is how I learned harmony. It was innate until I was in fourth grade and grew tired of singing in unison with the school choir. One day I started singing alto, much to the dismay of the choir teacher. Irritated, he asked, "Who's singing harmony?" I raised my hand and was asked to stop. Mom was infuriated after I told her what happened, and she went to talk to this teacher and suggested he not hold me back because I exceeded his expectations. Not long after that incident, Mom started training my voice.

Mom didn't accompany me in my early solos. I was in first grade when I sang a verse on "Jacob's Ladder" with the children's choir at church. Mrs. Grant taught that to me and played piano when I sang it. Mrs. Norman in Denver taught me "God Put a Rainbow in the Sky" when I was seven.

Before that, I usually sang along from the pew or with Dad and the car radio, or with my parents' records. Recently, I was riding in Dad's car and Journey's "Open Arms" came on the radio. Dad said, "You used to sing that song at the top of your lungs!" Anita Ward's "Ring My Bell," Stacy Latisaw's "Angel," and Dionne Warwick's "I'll Never Love this Way Again" were a part of my repertoire, too, before I could read. The latter two were songs I learned while watching my parents slow dance to them.

Grandma, Mom's mother, was really my first vocal coach. She and I would sing for hours while she and Granddad babysat me when Mom and Dad had to perform with God's Way. Grandma would play hymn after hymn on the piano and sing them to me. Then she'd encourage me to sing along. I can still feel the fluorescent piano lamp shining on our faces in the dark living room while grandma's wrinkled fingers would softly hit the keys and I would vigorously swing my legs on the stool from excitement. Those moments are the reason I will always have an unshakable fondness for hymns.

Sometimes Grandma and I would pretend we were a choir and march down the narrow hallway of her and Granddad's U-shaped house, singing. Our laughs would echo, bounce off the walls, and egg us on for encores!

Mom's sessions with me came a few years later and turned into more solos and, eventually, duets with Dad.

Dad is a classically trained tenor with a flawless falsetto and a penchant for creating the most beautifully complex harmonies.

Mom usually didn't play when Dad and I sang together. We often used a backing track instead, while watching Mom beam from the audience. For a while, our flagship song was "Somewhere Out There" by Linda Ronstadt and James Ingram from the animated movie, *An American Tale.*

When I reached my late teens, Mom started training my voice mostly when I asked her to. She never forced me to do anything musically, just as Dad never forced me to do anything artistically. I think they both knew if I wanted to do it badly enough, I would ask them.

When I was in sixth grade, I thought I wanted to learn piano. Mom bought a lesson book for me and started teaching me the basics, but I quickly grew disinterested. I think it was because I felt like the piano was Mom's instrument, not mine.

Mom and Dad's freedom with their artistic abilities intrinsically inspired me as a writer. When Mom would hear a song and a piano was nearby, she'd instinctively pick the tune out on the keys. She always picked new songs up quickly by ear and once she got it, she would immediately add her own twist to it. She always had music in her head and composed many songs. Sometimes the music came first, other times it was the words, but both could come simultaneously. She kept a cheap recorder nearby so she would remember what she'd done and a notepad and pen on the piano so she could write corresponding notes over the lyrics she composed. Many of her creations were used in all the recitals she did over the years, but she never told anyone she wrote them.

Mom always let me bring a mix tape that I'd made when we would ride somewhere. When it would play, she would either ask, "Is that Prince?" (to which my answer was usually yes) or she would say, "That's nice." It meant a great deal for my musical tastes to gain the approval of such an amazing musician like my Mom. She liked nasty songs, too. Most times she didn't know the words and I'd ask, "Mom, do you know what they're saying?" She'd say, "No, but I love that beat!" and she'd scream and do some spastic movements. If we were in the car, she'd turn the volume all the way up and roll the windows down until the song went off.

# SWEETS

Mom used to buy these huge peppermint sticks. She had a difficult time finding them after the Christmas holiday, but she would still hunt them down occasionally, buying three or four at a time.

Her method for eating one was brilliant: she'd take a hammer and go down the length of the stick until it was a mass of red and white chunks. Then she'd put them in a plastic sandwich bag that she'd place in her purse.

It would sit amid the other items that made her bag a convenience store with a shoulder strap. It held cough drops, lotion, fingernail clippers, aspirin, a mini notepad and pen, even a paperclip or two and enough tissues to satisfy a congregation. Those tissues always held the scents of all the other items in her purse. For the lotion, she'd reuse a bottle with a tan body and red twist-off cap. I think it originally housed some expensive moisturizer she bought from a department store a long time ago. When it would become empty again, she would fill it back up with fresh Vaseline Intensive Care lotion.

Eventually her selection of candy expanded to include Trident Plen-T-Packs of spearmint or peppermint chewing gum, Super and Dubble Bubble gum, Life Savers, and Mentos.

Mom had a strategy for eating gum, too. For the chewing gum, she'd take four or five sticks out at a time, putting each in her mouth one at a time. For the bubble gum, she'd take two pink masses and smash them together between her index finger and thumb before chewing on them. When I asked her why she did that, she said her mouth was too big for just one piece.

When she was finished, she'd sit the huge pink or gray mass on top of all the open papers that once wrapped around the gum in its original form.

She had different-sized purses and would get creative with packing all her goodies in the smaller ones. Sometimes they would have odd bulges, like they'd lost a fight with a baseball bat, but Mom didn't want to leave anything out that someone might want or need.

She'd even put enough packs of Mentos and Life Savers in her bag so she could give them away. Restless children in church often benefited most from that act. Mom would reach across pews and hand them the piece of candy she thought would keep them occupied. She had a knack for always picking the right flavor or consistency.

She kept more snacks in the back seat of her car, what she called her "diabetic snacks," just in case her blood sugar dropped. But even those were handed out to children she gave rides home to after choir rehearsal or adults who just wanted something to chew on.

Mom's own favorite sweets were York peppermint patties, 5th Avenue candy bars, and Chick-O-Sticks. Getting the York patties and 5th Avenues wasn't too difficult for her. She could get those in the checkout line at the two grocery stores she frequented. But she had to search every Mom & Pop pony keg until she found the Chick-O-Sticks. Sometimes I would accompany her on these trips. Once she struck gold, she'd buy an entire box just so she'd have her own supply if the pony keg decided to stop selling them.

The minute the weather would warm up, our favorite Dairy Queen in Woodlawn, Ohio would open for business. That Dairy Queen is the backdrop for many of my fondest childhood memories. When I was a little girl, that was one of the only perks my parents could afford to treat me to. Dad and I would go there and he'd order my vanilla ice cream cone or Cherry slushie. I'd stand on my toes and get a whiff of the hot air blowing the smell of syrup out of the screened service windows while Dad swatted bees away from me.

When I became an adult, Mom and I would swing by just to get an ice cream cone. We would be sitting in her apartment watching TV, when I'd say, "You know what I'm craving?" Mom would look at me and grin, knowing I would answer my own question. "A vanilla ice cream cone from Dairy Queen." She'd say, "Let's go," abruptly turn the TV off, throw the remote on the couch, grab her keys, and we'd head south on Route 4. It was so amusing to watch Mom drive with one hand while attacking her large vanilla cone. She'd say "I'll pay for this later" between each anxious lick.

There would be anticipatory silence until we stuffed the last bit of the cake cone in our mouths.

# FOOD

To eat Mom's food was to feel like you were being hugged from the inside out. It never made me feel sick or stuffed, and if I was sick before I ate it, putting her food on my tongue was the antidote.

Many of the dishes she prepared were influenced by her own mother, but she put her own spin on them. I find myself doing the same thing now. I may prepare baked chicken like Mom, but I use different seasonings.

Mom always said she cooked with love, and that's why what she prepared tasted like clouds melting on your chest or warm kisses on your stomach.

She didn't believe in substituting butter with margarine or generic brand ingredients with brand-name ones. "When you use off-brand, you can taste the difference," she would say.

There are certain tastes and scents I still only associate with Mom's cooking.

I would always beg to taste the batter for her lemon meringue pies. It always fascinated me how the lemon peels I

35

sometimes helped her grate disappeared in that batter, making the end result ecstasy on my tongue! I would squeal and moan as I licked the dripping spatula while Mom would just stare at me, wrinkle her forehead, and shake her head, saying "You are so silly."

Then I'd beg to help her snap the green beans or mix icing. As a little girl, I had no desire to know Mom's cooking secrets. I preferred to be delighted by whatever surprise she put on a plate for me to eat. I thought the experience would be anti-climactic if I knew what special effects she used.

The recognizable scents came at different times of the day.

The ones for breakfast were alarm clocks. Bacon made my eyes open. Sausage made me smile. The sounds of utensils hitting pots and pans made me get out of bed. I would usually stand in the kitchen, out of the way, and watch Mom finish up. There'd be a paper towel next to the stove on which she'd put the bacon.

During my time with her, she never had plates or cookware that matched or all those neat containers that serve a purpose for every kind of food. So Mom would just use what she had. She'd put all the things she cooked in her mismatched dishes, sometimes clanging them about until she found the ones she could tolerate the most.

She understood the importance of presentation, but the taste and temperature of the food meant so much more to her. Because of that, she didn't stay embarrassed for long about her odd dishes. Besides, no one who ever ate her cooking said, "These serving dishes don't match"; they always said, "This food is so good, Miss Gladine!"

I don't remember Mom ever calling me into the kitchen when she cooked. She never forced her children to do things they didn't want to do and I guess she figured if I wanted to learn how to cook, I would ask her how.

I did.

As an adult, I spent plenty of long-distance minutes asking Mom how to make homemade macaroni and cheese, beef and vegetable soup, or whatever else I could think of.

Her instructions on how to cook something always came out in a conversational way. She would even walk me through the grocery store, telling me where to find the not-so-obvious ingredients or what substitutes to use if I can't find a specific item.

She rarely measured anything. Everything she did to cook the food was instinctual, which taught me the real meaning of organic.

She'd say things like "... about as much as that first part of your index finger, it's enough." Even when Mom did measure, she was never meticulous about it. When she was following a recipe from a cookbook or magazine, she'd fill up a measuring cup without really looking at the lines on it. If it was water, she'd fill up the cup rather roughly, with the water splashing about. If it looked like it was too much, she'd casually dump some of it out until the level looked about right. She'd been cooking since she was a little girl, so she used her eye to dictate correct amounts, not a drawn line. She was the complete opposite of a new cook who lines everything up, putting that measuring cup on a flat surface to make sure the liquid is even with the one-cup line after it stops crashing against the sides.

I wanted to be a ready-made pro like Mom in my early days of cooking. My attempts left me with cuts on my fingers and hands that left permanent scars, and a burn mark on the side of my mouth, a reminder of the one time I didn't wait for the boiled potato wedges to dry before I tried to fry them.

Mom would always ask what kind of food I wanted to eat before I'd visit her. Unless I said otherwise, she'd cook my favorite meal: baked chicken, collard greens, and macaroni and cheese. She'd also get my favorite breakfast foods and fruit juices.

She even cooked greens for me after my period, to replenish the iron I'd lost during my cycle.

She didn't understand a lot of the foods I liked to eat, especially bagels and burritos. She'd refer to bagels as "that hard bread." When I'd get to her apartment, she'd say, "I got that hard bread you like," which always made me laugh.

Mom would wince when I ate a burrito in front of her, saying, "All that rice." She didn't understand foods like bagels and burritos. They were not a part of her segregated West Virginia childhood. Where she was from, rice went with gravy and liver, not black beans. She always said she'd eaten more than enough rice during her childhood and couldn't stand it as an adult. Mom grew up eating chicken and pork chops for breakfast, necessary foods to sustain enough energy to work mountainous farmland. She didn't have food choices as a child either. What was placed before her was what she had to eat. I guess by the time she became an adult, she refused to eat anything she didn't want to, including bagels and burritos.

She loved wraps, though. I think she first had one during a trip she took to Columbus, Ohio. She was the coordinator for a seniors volunteer tutoring program at an elementary school called STARS: Seniors Teaching and Reaching Students. Part of her responsibility was to go to these meetings every once in a while. She despised those trips, but one time, she and some of the other volunteers stopped at a restaurant that served wraps. She called me after she got home, excitedly asking, "Have you ever had a wrap?" I hadn't at that point. Mom liked telling me about things with which I was unfamiliar, so she went on to explain what they tasted like, concluding with "I really like them. I think I could make those."

Her other favorite meal was a chicken cordon bleu sub, fries, and lemonade from Penn Station. There was one down the street from where she lived and every time I came to visit, we'd both get the same meal and enjoy it together. Mom always had this bashful way of asking me if I wanted to go to Penn Station. She knew our favorite meal from there wasn't conducive to her diabetic diet and she'd always add to her request, "I'll pay for eating this later," as she enjoyed each overindulgent bite.

# AGE

I don't remember the exact day I realized Mom was getting old. That awakening probably happened in stages, like seeing her lose her balance, or her memory getting worse.

There's one vivid picture I have in my mind of Mom sitting at her post on the living room couch where she'd wait for me to arrive safely from my drive from Atlanta. This particular day was cloudy, but no matter what the sky looked like, Mom loved natural light, so she'd keep the blinds open until sunset. I don't know if it was the gray coming through the window or what, but when I walked through the door, Mom looked seventy. It wasn't a you-look-good-for-seventy either. It was a tired seventy. Like she was fighting to hang on to life. Her hair had started thinning considerably, a trait she inherited from Grandma, but was accelerated by her worrying and also probably from her secret health battles. Her eyes had lost their light, her skin didn't glow anymore, and her posture's confidence was gone.

She had also adopted a downtrodden laugh.

Mom had always had a hearty laugh, one that started in her belly, exploded in her chest, and shot out of her mouth! Sometimes she would laugh so hard, she'd cry and fall over. Then, during her recovery from the laughter, she would sit back up, get the last few chuckles out in between catching her breath, then grab her stomach.

The new laugh was unrecognizable, not even a shadow of the former one. It was reduced to a noise that came from the back of her throat, a kuh-kuh-kuh-kuh weighed down by grief. Her old laugh would've killed that grief, but I guess she no longer had the strength or desire to use it as a weapon against her sadness over being alone and disappointed in her older years.

Mom had always defied her age. Most of my life, people had a difficult time guessing how old she was. She would always attribute that to having a young husband and giving birth to a baby when she was in her forties.

But by the time this new laugh entered the picture, her young husband was no longer with her and her baby was an eight-hour drive away.

Her hands had become a dead giveaway of her age and she was quite insecure about them. They were weathered and wrinkled from years of service and neglect. I always thought it intriguing that Mom took such good care of the skin on every part of her body except her hands and feet. But that made perfect sense because she used those body parts to serve so many people and didn't make time to do things like get a pedicure or rub lotion on her hands after washing dishes.

The wrinkles that overtook her hands also indicated how weak they'd become. Those superhuman hands that once healed, nourished, and soothed had become so decrepit. She had even lost the feeling in some of her fingertips. The arthritis in them worsened in the last few years of her life and she had a very hard time doing the simplest of tasks like writing with a pen. When I would hold her hands, it felt like I was protecting them from being crushed by a breeze.

Despite her physical state, Mom always found time to exercise. During most of my childhood, she walked religiously. When she moved to an apartment complex that had a fitness room, she used it quite often. She would say some days she forced herself to go, to help relieve her depression and arthritic pain.

Mom's knees were really bad and walking up stairs was laborious. When I'd walk behind her, I'd put my hands under her butt, thinking it would relieve some of the pressure on her knees. She always said it helped, but I don't know if she meant it helped physically or it helped to know I was behind her if she fell.

Nine months before she died, she spent a week and a half with me in Atlanta. At the time, I was living in an apartment that was up several steps. For the first time in years, I saw Mom go up and down a staircase with little effort! I don't know if she made herself go up the steps like that so I wouldn't worry, or if she really did feel a new surge of energy that enabled her to conquer them.

I was always aware my time with Mom was limited. It wasn't something I told myself everyday, but it forced me to inadvertently overvalue my time with her.

Mom always joked that because she was in her forties when she had me, she wouldn't live to see me graduate high school or that she'd attend the commencement with a walker and a hearing aid. But she was there, cheering louder than anyone. Then she joked she wouldn't live to see me graduate college, but she was still alive for that, too.

Two life events she and I always spoke of in future tense were my wedding day and what kind of mother I would be.

Mom and I would discuss the gown I'd wear, where the wedding ceremony would be, whom I would invite and, of course, how I'd wear my hair. "Please wear your hair down, Devin," Mom would beg. "Not in a bun! Please don't pull it back or up."

She'd tease me about being a strict disciplinarian when I become a mother. "Your poor kids," she'd joke. "But they're gonna be so gorgeous and smart!"

I think Mom was so thankful she was alive for so many special moments in my life that she didn't want to get cocky and think she'd be around for all of them. She may have been doing all that teasing and projecting to prepare herself for her death, but she was also preparing me for it and giving me plenty of humor to distract me from being sad when those events happen without her physically being around for them. Mom did an incredible job of fattening my already healthy imagination while simultaneously exposing me to the reality that our time together was precious.

She cushioned the blow of her not being there for these events, because she placed herself in the picture a long time ago. I recently realized she never said, "On your wedding day, I'll ..." or "When you have children, I'll ..." It was always "I can see you now, Devin ..."

# SILENCE

We didn't say much to each other in her final days. We just did a lot of staring. Mom's face didn't look as aged as it had before she went to the hospital. Her skin was smooth and soft, despite her not having access to her favorite lotions and facial scrubs. I can imagine her inner monologue during those days in intensive care: Where is my Oceanus perfume oil from the Body Shop?

Mom's hair hadn't been washed since she'd been admitted. Many of the gels that had been used to insert whatever tubes were going into her body had caked up and hardened on her ends. One day, I asked a nurse if there was any way we could shampoo Mom's hair, and we did. There was such relief on Mom's face. She used to love to go to the salon and get her hair done. Her favorite part was the shampoo. She would always talk about how the hand strokes that lathered the shampoo and the warm water falling over her scalp soothed her.

Her vocal chords had suffered under the weight of the tube that was stuck down her throat for the ventilator. When it was taken out, her voice was boomless. It had been replaced by a whimper that came from the back of her damaged throat.

That ventilator didn't come out when it was supposed to.

I was sitting by Mom's bedside one day when she started sweating heavily and gagging. I went to the nurse's station and told them, then I stood outside Mom's room as about four nurses pulled a curtain and mumbled things. I heard one of them say, "Okay, Ms. Parrish." Then nothing. The curtain opened up, and one of the nurses held a tube. She said, "We hadn't planned to take this out for another week or so, but apparently your mom had other plans." The tube was stopped up with Mom's phlegm. The mass of mucous and spit looked like a blood-filled blob version of those multiple sticks of gum Mom used to chew.

When I went back to Mom's room, she was grinning victoriously. It was as if she'd had some secret plan to get that tube out of her throat so she could speak again. She did, too. Immediately. She was somewhat incoherent from a traumatic month of an extreme surgery and all the gases and medicines that had run through her veins. But she was cognizant enough to ask me why I wasn't at work. Even in her disoriented state, she didn't want me to worry about her.

By evening, I tried to get her mind back on her normal at-home routine, so I turned the TV on in time for her to watch Wheel of Fortune and Jeopardy. She called out a few letters during Wheel of Fortune, and during Jeopardy, she was especially eager about a category on painters. She answered "Van Gogh" at one point, but the answer was Picasso. I smiled, thinking of how she was putting all the stuff she learned during Dad's art school days to use.

I sat in her hospital room staring at her, trying not to lose her mind. Her voice wasn't the same, but the determination behind it was very familiar. She wasn't going to lose her mind, even as she was losing her battle.

By the next morning, she was back to commenting and laughing at the "idiots" making ridiculous wagers on The Price is Right.

Her arms had lost a lot of their strength, and the only part of them she could move without much effort was her forearms. Between asking me why I wasn't at work and where her car was, she would look at me, smile and pat my hand, hold it, then nod her head. Mom didn't have much longer to live and she was assuring herself that I'd be okay without her here on earth and she could leave when she was ready.

Indescribable peace washed over our silence. There were no last-minute I-love-yous or did-I-ever-tell-yous. Our relationship was never last-minute; it was always in the moment. Whenever I thought to thank Mom for anything, I called her and did it. If I was upset with Mom about something, I addressed it while the irritant was still warm.

A few years ago, Mom brought up a particular incident during which I confronted her when I was thirteen. Mom said I told her, "Mom, you think you're perfect. You never say you've done anything wrong." She said she didn't get mad at me for saying that because, after I said it, she realized I was right.

It's scary to have an adult relationship with your parents, but God bless Mom and Dad for allowing me to do that. Our silences were never awkward because the noise-filled times were so productive.

If Mom had miraculously walked out of that hospital, we would have just carried on in more noise and more silence.

# PHONES

When I was away at school, I could always count on a message from Mom being on my answering machine when I got back to my dorm room. They were always hilarious, too. She'd talk about anything, from telling me who she'd run into at the grocery store to telling me how she accidentally hit the closed caption button on the TV remote and needed my help to "get that writing off the screen."

Other times it would be her asking how to change the time on the VCR: "Daylight Savings is this weekend and I need you to tell me how to change this clock on the VCR.... Who invented Daylight Savings anyway and why do we have to do this twice a year.... No one asked for my vote when deciding to do this (click)."

After I moved to Atlanta, Mom would sometimes call me more than once a day. Because I worked overnights, I slept during the day. Before I fell asleep, I'd turn my phone's ringer off. When I'd wake up, there'd be at least one or two messages from Mom. She'd always start off her messages, saying things like "I'm glad you didn't pick up ..." or "Good, I'm glad you're sleeping ..." then tell me about a crazy encounter she had with one of her siblings or something as simple as a joke from one of her favorite reruns that made her laugh. Then she'd end her call with phrases like "I really need to get a life" or "I'm pitiful." I often saved those messages and would amuse myself with them later, playing them over and over to memorize them.

I always called her back when I woke up and reenacted her message. She'd laugh and ask, "Did I say that?"

# LETTERS

I've kept most of the letters and cards Mom sent to me during and after my college years. I even kept her one and only e-mail to me.

Mom loved sending cards to people. Her specialty was sending birthday cards, something she'd done since she was a little girl. As she got older, she kept a planner with everyone's birthdates noted. She would buy her cards in bulk, months in advance as she remembered. Some had specific messages for specific people, while others were thank-you cards or nondescript cards she'd find a future purpose for or she'd set aside for a perfect stranger.

She also sent cards to newlyweds to encourage them in their marriage and couples who made it to a thirty-year or more anniversary to applaud such personal landmarks.

Mom's cards or letters always arrived at the best times, usually when I was having the third worst day of my life in a week. On days when I'd had a disagreement with a professor or was especially homesick, there'd usually be an envelope from Mom's special stationery leaning in my mailbox, which always made me grin before I even put my key in to unlock it. Sometimes there were birthday cards inside which would always arrive at least three days before my actual birthday and other times they were just "thinking of you" notes.

She'd always put the date and time she was writing her note in the letter or card: "It's Sunday 6:15 P.M." or "This is Friday Morning at 7:30." She refused to get rid of her typewriter, and the more her fingers succumbed to arthritis, the more she relied on it. But she eventually embraced a laptop she received from the volunteer program for which she was a coordinator. When she was given the iBook, she started using odd fonts and colors to type her letters, which was amusing to see. The letter would start in a tame black font and be a different size and color by the time it ended.

Mom's mail was also how she'd send me extra cash and at times, all that would be in a card or folded piece of paper would be a twenty-dollar bill or money someone from church gave her to give me. She'd always write some kind of quick "Love, Mom" or "This is all I could spare this time" inside to personalize it. She would also stick an article she'd oddly cut out of a magazine or newspaper about an actor I liked or some political issue and stick it inside the envelope, just before she sealed it.

When I moved to Atlanta, her notes came more frequently. That move was for real. It wasn't seasonal like college when I'd return for breaks. The move to Atlanta meant I wouldn't be moving back in with her or staying for an extended period of time like a whole summer.

In her letters to me after I moved, she would tell me how much she missed me or how she woke up and forgot I didn't live with her anymore. I'd cry reading those cards and letters, imagining her walking past my empty room, looking at the wooden "D" she'd placed on the door with furniture glue.

I'd commit her words from that mail to memory, trying to make some kind of long-distance conversation out of them. One that would resemble the random exchanges we had when I was still a room away.

# GIFTS

There were several instances during my junior and senior years where I had especially bad days at school. I didn't have my own car and had to ride the bus for all four years of high school. That didn't bother me so much, but when you have a bad day and your solace from it is at home, the bus ride further delays the moment you can collapse on your bed and cry.

Mom had stopped working a forty-hour workweek by the time I reached middle school. It was an agreement she and Dad reached, one they thought would be best considering the catapult I made from elementary sixth grade to middle school sixth grade when we moved to Ft. Wayne.

On one particular day, when I finally got off the bus and reached home, Mom was there. She only asked "How was your day?" when I walked in. I answered, "Terrible, Mom," as I rushed to throw my backpack in my room. There on my bed was a wonderful surprise: new clothes and a new pair of shoes! I spun out of my room and ran back to the living room, wrapped my arms around Mom and squealed, "Thank you, Moooooom!"

It was a black-striped gray pants suit and black loafer mules with laces. It was my style at the time and proof that Mom was so good at picking out clothes for me.

My whole life, Mom was great at getting the most appropriate gifts for me. Whether it was a Nancy Drew mystery or blush, it always complimented where I was in my life.

After moving back to Cincinnati from Gastonia, I had to live with my Aunt Janice so I could attend the high school where my dad and Parrish aunts and uncles attended. My parents were living at my grandparents' house with Grandma and Aunt Liz in a different part of town. I had to sleep on the couch in Aunt Janice's living room. It was difficult sleeping in an unpredictable environment where I never knew which friend my cousin Kris would bring through the front door.

Mom was aware of my discomfort, but she was also proud of my patience, so she would reward me with a pair of earrings or a unique pair of shoes or a dress.

When we finally got an apartment, Mom bought a brass daybed for me. It was the first real bed I'd had in years. She bought several throw pillows and sprinkled them all over the bed. She was giving me a glamorous bed on a minimal budget and she knew I'd think it was the most marvelous thing I'd ever seen.

Mom always promoted the use of perfumes and scented lotions. She had her favorites over the years: Jean Nate, Halston, Colors by Benetton, and for years she bought Juba oil from the Body Shop until it was discontinued. I don't think Mom ever took a shower in my lifetime. She was all about the bath: Calgon bath beads and Dawn liquid soap, which she swore made the best and longest-lasting bubbles.

She helped me discover Chantilly when I reached middle school, which was my favorite until I got into Exclamation and

Debbie Gibson's Electric Youth, mostly because of their cool bottle designs.

I kept all my cosmetics in the bathroom I shared with my parents. When Mom would see that my Chantilly was running low, she'd surprise me with a new bottle. She often bought the gift set for me that included the lotion and perfume. She always thought of me in a big way, even when she was out getting something small for herself.

I was twenty-four when I got my first car, so I'd spent most of my life on public transportation or other people's vehicles. In high school, it was never an ordeal for me to get access to my parents' cars. If I wanted to drive to school in Dad's car, I'd drive him to work in order to keep it. On weekends, Mom would usually get her errands out of the way in the morning so I could have the car for the afternoon and evening. I never abused their trust, and because of that, I also had my own key to their cars.

One time when Mom's car was in the shop, the loaner she got was a Volkswagen Jetta. I had to work as a ticket-taker at a football game one night, and she let me drive it to the field. I was so happy because so many of my classmates saw me driving in it! Mom wanted me to experience the thrill of having something I wanted, even if it was for just a few hours.

She always wanted to give me more and would say, "If I had a Porshe, Devin could drive it."

I didn't envy my peers' sweet sixteen cars and Winter and Spring Break trips. Many of them were given these things without earning them and were just as unhappy upon receiving them as they were before the fact. Most importantly, none of them had the character I had from not getting everything I wanted. The gifts I received weren't things I thought I deserved; they were surprises my parents thought I should have.

# HAIR

Before I first asked Mom to straighten my hair, I had mounds of dark brown curls and deep waves that only a marine like my mom could navigate. My hair probably helped take a huge chunk of the life that was left in her arthritic hands when I was born.

She used to breathe heavily when she'd comb and brush through my hair. It wasn't the kind of breath I could feel on the back of my neck, it was the kind of breath that never left the back of her throat; it just pressed against it, making a hhhh-hhhh sound.

For a long time, the tools she used to do my hair were: a cup of water, Jergens lotion, comb, brush, and four throw pillows from the couch that would rest on the floor between her banister-like legs. Mom would sit above me in an armchair in our makeshift beauty salon that would collapse after she put the last ribbon in my hair.

Sometimes we'd talk while she did my hair. I'd talk about how complicated my homework was or how I was not looking forward to dealing with certain schoolmates. Other times the only voice would be Mom's telling me when to turn so she could twist another braid.

When it was time to wash my hair, we'd go to the kitchen. I would strip down to my white t-shirt and panties and climb up on the counter so my hair would fall into the sink. Mom would always test the water temperature before getting my hair wet. Then she'd repeatedly ask, "It's not too hot, is it?" I'd say it wasn't and Mom would follow up with "You sure? That's pretty hot."

At that age, the feeling of having Mom's hands in my hair was love. The rushing water and shampoo was what "I love you" sounded like.

I always giggled uncontrollably when Mom washed my hair. Her fingertips on my scalp instantly brought goose bumps all over my body. Mom would always shake her head when I did this and say, "You are so silly."

When I was six years old, I cut a lot of my hair off after a girl in my first grade class told me my hair was ugly.

The night I did this, my parents were in the living room watching TV and I was in my bedroom. I was supposed to be asleep, but I sneaked into the kitchen and got a paper grocery bag and the scissors. Then I went back in my room, closed the door, took down the braids Mom had put in my hair that morning, and started cutting. I put each curly chunk in the bag, and when I was finished, I simply put the scissors next to the bag and went to sleep.

The next morning, my parents came to wake me up. Mom was sitting on the edge of my bed. Dad was standing in the doorway. I had forgotten that I'd altered my look the night before until I saw the look on my parents' faces. Then I looked over at the bag next to my bed overflowing with hair. Mom found the whole scene amusing and was laughing when I woke up. Dad was twenty-seven at the time, so he had a very youthful reaction to my new look. He frowned like someone had stolen his most prized possession. After I told him why I'd cut my hair, he, in a very dad-like way, said, "If somebody told you your head was ugly, would you cut that off, too?" Mom, on the other hand, was fifty, so me cutting my hair was comical to her. There was probably even something in my act that reminded her of the time she cut off her hair as a girl.

My hair was several different lengths, so Mom took me to a professional salon to get it cut evenly. Secretly, Mom was probably relieved she didn't have to tackle as much hair every morning. On the way to the salon, Mom explained that the girl who told me my hair was ugly was jealous and still would be even though my hair was a lot shorter.

I didn't really understand jealousy at that age because I was so busy trying to appease. I figured everyone should like each other, so if I possessed something that was unpleasant to someone else, I should get rid of it. So, to answer Dad's question, yes, I probably would've tried to cut my own head off if someone told me it was ugly.

By the time I started second grade in Denver that fall, my hair had gone from being a mass of stubby curls to long enough to put into two medium-length ponytails. That's just how Mom styled my hair for my class photo, along with bangs and two purple ribbons to match the argyle vest and pleated skirt I wore.

Mom's collection of ribbons had grown significantly, and rarely a day went by that I didn't have one in my hair. She was giving me a signature style even before I could put my clothes together well. I never lost a ribbon, either.

They stayed in my hair until Mom took them out before I went to bed. Mom's love affair with my hair began with those ribbons. Baby's breath was an alternative adornment, but only when I was a flower girl in a wedding.

When we moved back to Cincinnati, my fourth grade year was starting and so was my itch to dress myself. I needed options, one of which was the opportunity to style my hair in different ways that having curly hair didn't allow me to. So Mom magically pulled out a hot comb and started pressing my hair.

I anxiously sat on a bar stool in the kitchen the first time she straightened my hair, having graduated from the throw pillows.

It was a bit intimidating to see a metal comb get red hot on a stove, but I trusted Mom would use it with safe results. She took it off the eye, blew on it, and patted it on a kitchen towel. She told me to be very still as she made the first stroke through one of many sections she made in my hair. She created a monster with the final stroke. I immediately saw five hundred new styling options for my flatter hair: bangs that laid down and the use of a curling iron!

Mom was my personal, on-call stylist through the sixth grade. Then she became my occasional stylist, handling all straightening aspects and complicated 'do's that I didn't master like the upside-down French braid. By the time I got to middle school, Mom bought a footstool for me to sit on when she created masterpieces out of my strands or cut my ends.

There were others who touched my hair during those years. They were professionals, like Miss Liz in Ft. Wayne, Indiana who gave me perfect bangs and a flat look that framed my face; and then there was the woman who gave me my first bob before my senior year in high school.

I always went back to Mom.

Even after I was in high school and supposedly got too big for it, I'd still wind my body up on the kitchen counter when I wanted to feel Mom's fingertips on my scalp. I would giggle, too, just like I was five years old again, and sticking to the script, Mom would say, "Devin, you are so silly!"

I watched Mom go through her own hair changes during our time together. She had an afro when I was born, then she straightened it. During my toddler years, she'd wash her hair, section it, and put twist two French braids on both sides of her head. When I was nine, she had a bad professional coloring that turned her hair magenta and she never let a stylist color her hair again.

Then, after years of having medium-length hair, she nervously asked my Uncle Greg to cut her hair with his clippers. Mom carried off the drastic cut with Dad's encouragement. I think he had more confidence in Mom's stateliness than she did. She wore that buzz cut for a while and, like her favorite fragrance from the Body Shop, it became her trademark. A couple of her sisters followed in her footsteps and got the same cut, but they didn't carry it off for long.

Because of her own ability to let her guard down, she encouraged every outrageous, schizophrenic style I created on my own, particularly when I was in high school, which is when I was at my freakiest. One day I'd wear plaits, another day it would be wild and fanned out waves. Whatever it was, Mom thought they were all beautiful expressions of my creativity and her support fostered that.

When I started wearing my hair naturally again during and a few years after college, a behemoth of curls reminiscent of the ones Mom used to tackle reappeared on my head. She would often moan under her breath looking at them, probably thinking how thankful she was she didn't have to manage them this time.

She was with me when I decided to get a relaxer. When the process was over, my hair ran down my back like a calm river. Mom yelled when we walked out of the salon. I just smiled. Mom's nonverbal responses were always the best indicators of how she felt about something.

When I became an adult, Mom took to randomly running her fingers through my hair or playfully messing it up. When I'd go to church with her, she'd take my hair and throw it over the back of the pew, to which I'd respond, "Mooooom!"

Then there were the times I'd sit on the edge of her bed and watch TV with her while she laid down. Her hand would reach for my hair and tousle it. "All that hair," she'd say. Sometimes it would be a quick toss, sometimes she would push all of it up to the front of my head, making it fall in my face while she screamed.

I recently started coloring my hair, mostly to cover up all the gray I've had since college. After a hair stylist encouraged me to take a chance, I got blonde highlights and she cut my hair into a bob. I wore that bob for about nine months, then I asked the stylist to cut it even more.

As I write this, my hair now stands an inch and a half from my scalp. I've come full circle with my hair: last time my hair was almost this short, I cut it to make others feel comfortable. This time, I did it for me. I even went further in my cut than Mom did with hers. She always left a few long strands on the top, I suppose it was a compromise for making others feel comfortable, fearing how going that extra step would be perceived instead of completely following through.

# HANDS

I inherited Mom's long, thin fingers, but hers held magic cures and performed the most complicated surgeries.

When I was seven years old, the Denver apartment complex we lived in had a walkway near our building that had wooden banisters. My hand raked across those banisters once while I was playing outside and a splinter got lodged in my right middle finger's nail bed. I screamed and cried as I ran to our apartment, startling Mom. "What happened, Devin?" she asked half-scared, half-irritated. I screamed, "I got a splinter in my fingernail!" She said, "I need you to calm down, so I can get it out."

She disappeared, then reappeared with some tweezers. She sat me on the kitchen countertop and started digging at the back of my fingernail. I was a fussy patient, whimpering and shrieking every time she dug deeper, which made it more difficult for her to pull the splinter out. Frustrated, she looked in my eyes and, in a firm voice, said, "Devin, the more you fuss, the longer it's gonna take me to get the splinter out ... now hush!" That reduced me to silent tears. She wiggled that splinter out, then washed my finger with some mommy concoction so it wouldn't get infected. More than fifteen years later, I had to pull a splinter from Mom's fingernail.

She'd accidentally stubbed her right thumb on one of her dining room chairs with wicker backing.

She was in a lot of pain, which was magnified by her diabetes. She sat on the couch, holding on to her finger. It was strange to see Mom fazed by a seemingly minor inconvenience because, to that point, she'd always had a high threshold for pain.

By the time I got the tweezers, a little bit of blood started to form where the back of the nail meets the skin. "Just pull it out, Devin. Don't tug at it, just yank it out." I obeyed.

Afterward, I told her she should wash the wound, but she waved away my suggestion. Knowing Mom, she probably just waited until she washed the dishes and indirectly cleaned it out.

One of the first things I can remember I wanted to do like Mom was type. She was the fastest typist I'd ever seen or heard. The sound of her fingers hitting the keys of an IBM Select sounded like a deck of cards being shuffled.

A house in Wyoming, Ohio my parents rented for a short while had the most horrible wallpaper in it left behind by the previous owners. But we were too poor to do anything about it, so it stayed on the walls for as long as we stayed in that house. I think the furniture was left behind, too. I remember the big, dark wood dining room table that Mom's red typewriter sat on. She spent many hours on that machine, typing cover letters and resumes for Dad and lyric sheets for her gospel group, God's Way.

I would sit in front of it, watching Mom teach me how to put the typing paper in and set margins. I hadn't learned how to read yet, so I would just type mumbo jumbo hoping my rhythm was an exact match to Mom's.

It was on that same dining room table that Mom taught me how to write a check. "The cents go above the 100. If there are no cents, just put two zeros." I had no idea what she was talking about, but I remembered every word, never having to ask her for a refresher course when I got my first checkbook.

Her hands became so fragile in her older years. Her fingers would have these spasms, which began when she was still fixing my hair, but became worse long after she stopped. Her home-made cure was to run them under hot water.

She often complained that her hands exposed her age. She was right. They were the most wrinkled part of her because she never bothered to take care of them. She never had a manicure or put lotion on her hands after washing dishes. Actually, she never gave her hands a break. She cooked everything from scratch, never used a dishwasher, pounded the keys of a piano, took heavy wet clothes from the washer and folded them once they came out of the dryer. Doing my hair alone probably took years off of them.

Mom's hands also showed her nervousness. People often thought Mom wasn't shy because she was a musician and she was always helping someone or talking to strangers. But she did not like attention. She preferred sitting behind a piano, standing behind the wall of a kitchen, or cheering others on from the bleachers. She fidgeted with her hands a lot and if an object was in her hands, it became an extra tool in her fidgeting. She would also smooth the corners of her mouth profusely or unnecessarily run her index finger down the side of her nose.

Church bulletins with folded corners or remote controls with disfigured buttons and rubbed-off numbers were also evidence of her hyper fingers' destruction, destruction to release the pain of being paid attention to, painful attention because her belief was that the gifts she had and the power she possessed because of those gifts was not something she created; rather, she was the vessel through which God displayed His power. To be the possessor of such power—and for Mom, many of her superpowers were in her hands—was a gargantuan responsibility, one that Mom often didn't think she was capable of displaying in such a finite body.

# FREEDOM

Freedom is a little girl dancing in her underwear.

I never hesitated to dance when the spirit moved, because my mother encouraged me to. Whether it was theme music for a TV show or a commercial or a song ... I would immediately move my body with innocent abandon while Mom would clap and shout a "Go 'head, Devin!" as I moved.

There were even times when Mom was doing my hair and I would be compelled to move. She never once got upset that I'd ruined a perfectly straight part or that my wild movement unraveled a braid she'd just coaxed her arthritic fingers to twist. It felt like the world stopped just so I could dance. I realize now, it wasn't the world, it was Mom and she was my world.

Sometimes, I would dance improvised routines to entire songs. Other times, it would just be twirls and kicks for a moment. Then there would be those times when my parents would have company, and Mom would ask me to dance. I was chronically shy and most times I would protest. *They're not gonna get the way I move the way Mom does*, I thought. I never gave them the performances I gave my parents. I never danced in that out-of-body way in front of others the way I did in front of the two people who loved me most. So, when I did dance for others, they always got the commercial version, while my parents always got the avant garde.

There is no feeling in the world like being comfortable in your own skin. You don't care who's looking at you strangely because what you're doing isn't strange to you. Mom is the reason I feel that way now, because no matter how weird I may seem to others, her go 'heads are always in my head. I always imagine her somewhere in the room, cheering me on.

She wasn't just encouraging me to move my body; she also wanted me to let the Spirit move me, to laugh heartily, love hard, and turn the volume up really loud on a good song.

She encouraged me to wear my hair and clothes the way I wanted and sincerely trusted my judgment in those areas. She knew I wouldn't do anything that would be inappropriate or to my own detriment. She never asked, "You sure you want to wear that?" Instead, she said, "I like that!" I don't think she always liked everything I had on or everything I did to my hair. What I think she liked was watching me find my way as an individual in a harmless, original way. Not through sneaking out of the house, missing curfew, taking off in her car or experimenting with drugs or alcohol, but clothes, hair, and art.

I could leave the house in brown leather and wooden platforms and a crocheted vest, or silver clogs and a sweater dress or a hounds tooth blazer with black denim bellbottoms and burgundy low top canvas Converse with the confidence in knowing that no matter how I was ostracized at school for what I wore, Mom liked my style and that made me comfortable with liking it, too.

By the time I reached high school, I had stopped trying to fit in. I changed schools three times in three different states during my freshman year, and didn't care what judgments my classmates had for me. That attitude was reflected in my personal style. I started dressing and fixing my hair to express my individuality. I paid for it, too. My peers would snicker at my ensembles. It was the mid-90s and most of my peers were playing it safe with their clothes. They dressed to fit the role they played in predictable high school melodrama.

When the school day was over, I could return home, go to my room, do my homework, and then do the things I wanted to do: sing, dance, write, or just daydream. I could write something and read it to Mom or sing at the top of my lungs.

Mom would never tell me to be quiet. She enjoyed listening to me entertain myself, often stopping whatever she was doing to listen. Most of the time, my rants would only be interrupted by Mom's knock on the door with her asking, "Was that you or the album?"

# IN/DEPENDENCE

Mom served as my journal for years. There's a huge lapse in my entries when I was at the peak of communicating with Mom.

She bought me my first diary the summer before my fifth grade year. I wrote in it practically every day. Most of what I wrote about was boys I had crushes on or not fitting in. Subject matter got a little more complex when I started middle school the next year. I wrote about unfair grading and what my parents did that irritated me but I was still writing about not fitting in and having crushes.

Mom was the subject of many of my anti-parent tirades. There was one entry in particular in which I took jabs at her personality and physical appearance. I don't remember what disagreement I had with her that triggered it but when I stopped writing, I had covered two pages. I told Mom about it immediately after I wrote the final word. I was tearful and apologetic. Mom forgave me, quietly.

There was no punishment, no reprimand; she didn't even ask to see what I'd written. Afterward I scratched out every hurtful word, adding huge NOs in thickened ink on each page. It was a pivotal moment in our relationship. I'd always known I could tell Mom anything and I did. But it was in that moment that I knew I could keep telling Mom anything, even as I got older and my thoughts became more complicated.

That's exactly what I did. I still kept a journal all through high school and college, but my entries usually dealt with my peers, teachers, crushes, or sexual inclinations. Whatever grievances I had with my parents, I told them directly.

During the time my parents were breaking up, I became my mother's journal.

The summer of 1996, I got an internship at The Cincinnati Post. I would take the Metro downtown and Mom would drive me to the bus stop every morning. We'd sit in her car as I waited for the number 78 and I'd listen to Mom fight back tears as she talked about Dad and the woman he was leaving her for. Then, we'd see my bus coming and I'd get out of the car as Mom would say, "I shouldn't be dumping all this on you, Devin." and I'd say, "Where else are you gonna dump it, Mom?"

There's a downside to such human journaling. My dependence on Mom's emotional availability kept me from experiencing similar intimacies with other people. Actually, I didn't even have a desire to. My mentality was that I could always call Mom and cry or be completely myself and she would accept me without judging, teasing, or belittling what I felt.

I experienced such a rich life of love from two people, but instead of really sharing that love with other people, I hoarded it. Before Mom died, I'd never really cried out of vulnerability in front of anyone other than her or Dad. I often cried out of anger over being made fun of or misunderstood outside of my parents' company. I held back that part of myself with other people, assuming they would drop out of my life when they found out who I really was.

# PREMONITION

A couple months before she died, Mom was really urging me to visit her. It started about seven months after she'd spent a week and a half with me in Atlanta. Seven months was the longest stretch of time I'd ever gone without visiting Mom. In that time period, normally, I would've driven to Cincinnati at least once to spend a weekend with her.

No event had ever served as an excuse for me to visit. Many times, I wouldn't tell anybody that I'd be in town. I would drive to Mom's just so I could be at her feet and I didn't want anything or anyone to disturb that.

When someone would stop by, I'd usually be in Mom's bedroom with the door closed, still in my pajamas watching television. I would hear someone ask, "Is Devin here?" to which I'd roll my eyes because I didn't want to be bothered. Then I'd hear Mom say, "Yeah, she's in my room," and to keep whoever was stopping by from interrupting my seclusion, sometimes she would lie and add, "She's asleep."

It was March 2005 when Mom started asking, "When are you going to come see me?" That question was odd coming from Mom because she'd never had to ask it before. I would always call to tell her I had some time off and was going to come see her before she could even make the request.

I rarely won the holiday lottery at work, so it was understood that I probably wouldn't be home for Thanksgiving or Christmas. I would usually find time soon after the New Year to visit, but by this time I was two months overdue.

I was already getting a week off toward the end of April and had planned to see Mom.

Then Grandma Mattie died.

It was toward the end of March—on a Saturday—when my father's mother took her last breath. Mom called to tell me.

"Devin, Mattie died this morning," she said listlessly. She waited for my crying to die down before she said, "Call your Dad."

Returning for Grandma Mattie's funeral a week later would be the unofficial visit that allowed me to see my mom in a place other than a hospital, for the last time.

After Grandma's casket was closed and her body was carried to the hearse, Mom and I said goodbye to Dad. We did not attend the burial. Instead, me, Mom, my brothers Randy and Kenny, and my sister Kathy decided to meet at a restaurant for an early dinner.

Kenny left in his own car. Randy rode with Kathy. Mom rode in my car. The first restaurant we tried was closed so we tried another. On the way to that one, Mom started holding her stomach and moaning. As we passed the elementary school where I attended first, fourth, and fifth grade, Mom said breathlessly, "I have to go to the restroom."

She was concentrating on her breathing and I started to get angry with myself for not being able to build a restroom in the backseat of my car so she wouldn't have to wait. I asked, "You want me to stop at a gas station?" She said, "No. I can wait 'til we get to the restaurant."

I pulled up to the door of the restaurant where my older siblings were already waiting. Mom got out of the car and Kathy walked her inside.

She said she got some relief after using the restroom, but I think in that instance and many others Mom made light of her bad health so no one would make a fuss.

However she was feeling, Mom appeared to be in good enough spirits to laugh and joke with us. She ordered her own meal, ate a little bit off our plates, and ordered apple pie with vanilla ice cream. She ate all of it while maintaining this look of defiance on her face as she put the last piece of pie in her mouth. It was almost as if she was daring it to make her stomach act up again.

When I called Mom's physician to tell her Mom had died, she said, "Your Mom was a very sick woman."

I think Mom's options were told to her, but she chose to let her illnesses run their course. Her body had become a twenty-four—hour battlefield in which the manifestations of every burden she'd ever carried took the form of cancerous pancreatic tumors, high blood pressure, diabetes, diverticulitis, and whatever other ailments she never disclosed. I think, at some point, Mom realized there was no cure in all the medications she was taking; they were just delaying the inevitable.

She survived two years in a TB sanitarium during the early 1950s, never giving up on her life back then because she was excited about what was in front of her even while watching everyone around her die. But I think at some point she figured her earthly work was done.

That's why she interacted with me the way she did in those final days in her hospital room: the knowing grin on her face as she looked at me, the affirming nods, the hand-holding. She knew her time was at its shortest. She'd attended all the milestones in my life to that point, many of which she felt were unexpected bonuses.

# JETTISON

Mom allowed herself to become the physical container for everybody else's stuff, forsaking her own health and peace of mind. Sometimes I wonder if she would've lessened her health problems and prolonged her life had she not done that so much. The probable "yes" to that question angers me.

Sometimes I feel like Mom was just treated like a machine with strong hands to cook the perfect meal, fix hair, type a paper, wash clothes, play piano, clean, sew, heal ... whatever.

She always said she was born to be a wife and a mother. Perhaps she never felt whole after one role ended. What do you do when your children are all grown, self-sufficient, and don't need you anymore? I guess the way Mom coped with it was by drowning herself in other areas of service and in her two grandsons' lives. She was never defined by a job title as most folks are. She was defined by what she did for a living, which was serve. She was known for her gifts and how she used them. I think people had problems with her because she did many things well and wasn't afraid to admit when she was weaker in other areas.

She would always hold back so others could shine. But she didn't want me to do that. That's why she would tell me to wear my hair down and encourage me to dress the way I wanted to. She didn't want me to put my light under a bowl. I'm gradually getting there, but I, too, hold back sometimes. It's already lonely enough being gifted and smart; you don't want to alienate everybody because of it, too.

Mom gave her all to everybody and kept nothing for herself. I'm trying to figure out how to do a better balancing act in my own life.

One of the hardest "no's" I ever said in my life was to Mom. When I finished college and moved to Atlanta, Mom and I discussed the possibility of her moving to Georgia. The proposal was for me to either get a two-bedroom apartment or house to share with her, or for her to move into her own place on the outskirts of Atlanta, to a place she would feel comfortable driving around in and maintaining her familiar sense of independence.

Initially, my attitude was upbeat. I started slowly looking at housing and even kept an ear out for church musician openings. Everything was brewing for Mom's move down south, until she came to visit me in mid-August 2004.

We'd had a fantastic time together. Mom really enjoyed herself and got a real kick out of seeing her baby as an adult in a city that was completely unfamiliar to her. We watched movies, went to the mall, and I drove her around town. She kept saying, "It's so pretty here... . I can't get over all the trees!" Prince was in town for his Musicology Tour and I called her from Philips Arena, screaming as the Time opened the show and Dad stood next to me, smiling.

The next afternoon, we were watching random TV shows. Mom was stretched out on my couch with her usual snack: a Sprite and peanut butter on Ritz crackers. I remember feeling so satisfied that Mom was comfortable in my apartment. We had shared many afternoons and evenings that way when I'd take up temporary residence with her in between college breaks. This time, she was taking up temporary residence with me on her break from a life of kindness.

I was sitting in the rundown secondhand recliner that Dad bought for a studio he used to rent. He gave it to Mom when he moved out of that studio, and she gave it to me before I moved to Atlanta so I would have at least one chair to sit in.

Then, in the middle of all of our laughing and channel surfing, an awkward silence abruptly filled the room. Suddenly, Mom asked, "Devin, you don't want me to move here, do you?" I stared straight ahead, trying to coerce my tears to retreat.

I finally turned to look at her and answered, "No."

A bit disappointed, she said, "I knew it. I could tell." I quickly turned back around, knowing that while Mom wanted me to have my own life; I had just shattered part of her dream to perhaps start a new one.

At the same time, I knew that I would end up resenting her if she moved closer to me. We would've gone from having a relationship rooted in honest authenticity to having a depraved relationship in which I became a disgruntled caregiver who viewed Mom as a burden.

I was suddenly clairvoyant: Mom asking me how to get somewhere, then apologizing for asking, then me saying it was okay; then Mom not asking me something because she didn't want to get on my nerves and me feeling guilty about my obvious impatience. It was a future soaked with second-guessing, and Mom and I never second-guessed each other.

Dad drove Mom back to Cincinnati two days after Mom and I decided it was best that she stay there. From my apartment window, I watched Dad put Mom's bag in his car while Mom settled in the passenger's seat. I cried uncontrollably while watching Dad pull out of a parking space and asking God to take care of the only two people who loved me unconditionally.

I wasn't really sure it was Mom's dream to move to Georgia anyway. I felt like she was looking for a dream to have, an attempt to live life selfishly for once in her life. But where would she have fit in? Her ex-husband was living a foreign life with his second wife. Her baby daughter was an adult attempting to carve her own niche in a city that didn't know her mother or father's name. Would she have been able to make an identity for herself separate from ours, too? If she had moved to Georgia and become a musical director for some church, would that have helped to make her feel like she was starting a new life or continuing her old one in a new place?

I obsessed over the what ifs until I realized I had to let those go just like I had to let go of the guilt of knowing I would never be to Mom what she'd been to me.

# LOVE

She used to use my comb and brush when I would visit her. I would leave them on the bathroom sink counter and when I'd go to use them later, I would see her auburn hair woven between the bristles.

At the time, it annoyed me because I regarded those items as my stuff. But now I know she used some of my things because it was mine and she wanted to share in what belonged to me, even if it was as simple as using my brush and comb, two tools I used to take care of the hair she loved so much. It gave her goose bumps just to touch her scalp with something that had touched mine.

When you love someone, you do things like that. It's like wearing their jacket, sleeping in their shirt, spraying their cologne or perfume to share in something that's part of that loved one's essence.

When Dad and I went to visit Mom in the hospital while she was in a stupor, Dad opened the closet in her room and saw a jean jacket he gave her and some gray sneakers he'd bought for her. It made him cry in a way I'd never seen him weep before.

The jacket was one he'd given her off his back. During one of his visits to Cincinnati, he went to Mom's apartment wearing it. Mom saw it and said, "That's a nice jacket, Cos." Dad took it off and handed it to her. He'd ordered the sneakers for her online and had them mailed to her home. Mom called me when she got them and tried describing what they looked like over the phone.

"I've never had any shoes like these ... they look like Cos," she said.

She wore that jacket and those shoes like they were royal vestments. To her, they were because they came from the only man she'd ever truly been in love with. His scent was in that jacket; his taste was embodied in those shoes.

I never felt I was too much of an adult to rest my head on Mom's chest or stomach. I'd listen to her tired heart whisper its beats. Years of physical and emotional pain had taken a toll and I often wondered how it still managed to function.

Her stomach made sounds akin to fireworks launching every time I put my ear to it. I think Mom sensed I could hear the disharmony in her body. When my head would rest on her stomach, she would jokingly expand it in a rushed exhalation. We would both laugh, bringing my investigation to an abrupt end.

Our roles switched as we got older.

I loved taking care of my mother. I wanted to make her simple wishes a reality like she did mine. I wanted to pamper her and take care of her the way she did me. I wanted to be her superhero for a change.

We'd still walk hand-in-hand through the mall. One time when we were doing that, Mom said, "People probably think we're lesbians," and I giggled. Mom liked voicing other people's judgments aloud. I think as comfortable as she was in her relationship with Dad and me, she knew it made others uncomfortable. I think she was a little shy about the greatness of that relationship. She was nervous about being part of something so unique and God-given and for that to be misinterpreted by people who'd never experienced something like it.

My parents were the first two people I ever loved. With Mom gone, how do I transfer the new love I would've given her? Who gets that now? How is that distributed? How is such an abundant love for one person supposed to be rationed? Am I supposed to copy and paste it to everyone with whom I have meaningful relationships?

It's certainly not my job to keep all that love to myself. The greatest gift my parents have given me is their love. I can't quote verbatim any one thing either has ever said about love, but their examples of it are vivid in my subconscious.

# SEX

The summer after my fourth grade year, Mom and I used to go to Tri-County Mall in Springdale, Ohio to look at men's legs.

I don't remember how this pastime began, but I do remember it being fun and free. It usually started after Mom treated me to spaghetti from a food court restaurant called The Spinning Fork. When I was finished eating, we would walk over to a nearby bench and become spectators of perfect calves, tube socks be damned!

"Look look look look look look look look ..." Mom would say under her breath while tapping the side of my thigh so as not to bring attention to our secret recreation. "Nice legs, umph!" I'd sit beside her, giggling and blushing.

By the time I returned to school and began my fifth grade year, I had perfected the craft of eying the perfect legs among my peers.

I was used to Mom being in touch with her sexuality and she encouraged awareness of my own sexuality early in my life.

She told me I was sexy at age nine. What normal woman tells their preadolescent daughter she's sexy? The same woman who takes their daughter to the mall to look at men's legs.

She even told me I had the same sexy walk as my PaPa, my paternal grandfather. It would amuse her to watch PaPa and me walk side by side so she could compare our similar strides.

My parents and I never had "the talk" about sex, because sex was a natural topic of discussion. I knew about it before I even started first grade. Mom forbade me to use baby language when referring to mine or other people's body parts. There was no wee wee or pee pee. It was vagina and penis. My very conception and birth was controversial, but my parents didn't think I was too young for it to be explained to me.

My parents were affectionate in front of me. I have fond memories of them slow dancing, kissing, and holding each other's hands. I was somewhere in between it all and because of that, I knew what real intimacy looked like at an early age. It made me comfortable discussing even the most embarrassing things with them.

When I started developing breasts, my right one developed quicker than the left. I was ten years old and thought I had breast cancer. I immediately went to Mom and she touched my chest. I don't know if she thought something was wrong, too, but she already knew I was panicking so she stayed calm for me, probably praying the whole time that I was okay.

After a doctor's visit confirmed I was normal, Mom assured me I wasn't the first girl to develop one breast before the other and told me they would catch up with each other.

Three years later, I got my first period.

Mom, Dad, and I were moving from Ft. Wayne, Indiana to Gastonia, North Carolina. We made a stop at Grandma's house in Cincinnati on the way.

A lot had happened over the course of a few weeks. Dad lost his job in Ft. Wayne and he had no other financial choice but to accept the one in Gastonia. Days after I got my fall semester freshman class schedule in the mail, we had to pack up everything we owned and leave Ft. Wayne. Because of our abrupt move, I never got to experience the high school where I thought I'd spend my freshman year.

A day before we headed to Gastonia, I went to the bathroom and saw a copper-colored streak on my panties. I asked Mom to come in and I showed her. She said, "Oh, Devin!" and gave me a hug. Then she left to get some pads for me. She bought about three different kinds, hoping one brand would be to my liking.

It wasn't that Mom was happy I was going to have monthly cramps and bleeding. In fact, she was probably hoping I didn't inherit the horrible and at times debilitating cramping she experienced during the years she menstruated. I think she was relieved I had entered a certain stage of womanhood.

The very circumstances out of which I was born were strange. When Mom found out she was pregnant with me, people both inside and outside the medical profession offered her a bleak picture for my future. I think there was part of Mom that wanted me to belong to the normalcy of what girls experience, in defiance of those who cursed my very conception. I think she was overjoyed that she had a healthy child after having me with barely any prenatal care and at a late age. Maybe she was just happy my period finally came because I thought it never would.

I had a fall semester internship in Washington, D.C. during my junior year in college and came home during Thanksgiving break. While I was there, Mom and I attended a wedding to which I had worn a long red dress and matching heels. By the time we got to the reception, my feet hurt, so I changed into some flats. Mom and I were sitting in her car in the parking lot outside the reception hall. When I put my feet on the dashboard to change my shoes, Mom said, "Go 'head, Devin! You're gonna make your husband very happy one day!"

# REPETITION

Mom's senility began not long after I was born, but I benefited greatly from it. She would often repeat things, sometimes catching herself with an "Oh! I already told you that."

Other times, she wouldn't catch herself. If the short-temperedness of my speed-driven youth was on, I'd say "you already told me that." As I got older, though, those reruns became valued antidotes. I realized, through Mom's forgetfulness, she was inadvertently repeating things to me so I wouldn't repeat her mistakes. It also helped me build on the values that were instilled in her as a child.

Telling Mom about my everyday stresses and worries would often prompt her to say, "Don't repeat me." She attributed her poor health to all the things she carried—her problems and other people's problems. She didn't want me to believe in the myth that that's what women are supposed to do. She wanted me to do differently, to master the art of taking care of oneself and realize that that's humanly possible and doing so doesn't mean you're being selfish. Being on time is considerate; sitting in the middle of an empty pew so others don't have to step over you to sit down is considerate ... and humanly possible. What's not humanly possible is trying to solve everything in a finite body. That's God's infinite job: "Don't repeat me."

I had a panic attack before my final semester of college. I had basically gone nonstop for a year so I could finish in December 2000. I took twenty credits in the winter, then stayed for a summer semester. I came back to Cincinnati to stay with Mom for the rest of the summer, but even while I was there, I registered for an online literature class. Then, a few weeks before I was to return to school, I got word that I didn't have enough money to finish my last semester.

I tried not to worry about it, frantically scrambling to figure out how I could stir up $2,000 to solve my problem. But by the end of the day, I cried myself to sleep. I felt so defeated and disgusted that a couple thousand dollars were keeping me from reaching a goal I was so close to accomplishing.

Neither of my parents had extra money, no savings or mutual funds they could break the glass on in case of emergency. Most of my life, they only had right-now money. Asking other relatives was not an option, either. Many of them held a grudge against Dad for the way his relationship with Mom ended. They were also snickering at Mom for falling in love with a younger man, so I was indirectly punished as a result.

It was a cloudy August Saturday when I felt the shortness of breath. I tried to ignore it. Then I tried to make it go away on my own. I opened the sliding door in my room, allowing a breeze to come in. I thought I just needed some fresh air, but my breathing got worse. The door to my room was open, I was watching a movie I had rented, and I could hear Mom in the kitchen. My breathing got worse and I thought I was hyperventilating, so I went in the kitchen to get a brown paper bag without Mom seeing me. I returned to my room, sat on the floor by my bed, and started breathing into it, hoping Mom wouldn't see me.

It was early in the afternoon, but I already had on my pajamas: some faux-satin blue and white polka dot shorts and a faded Nutty Professor II t-shirt. That paper bag was doing absolutely nothing. "What a crock!" I said to myself and threw the bag on the floor. I was still trying to get a grip on my breathing but nothing I was doing worked.

The past year of my life to that point had finally caught up with me and my breathing was sounding an alarm. I was so busy trying to finish school by December, I'd begun overexerting myself to do it, registering for classes every semester, including summer, taking twenty credits at a time. At one point, I was working three jobs.

I was trying to die over a solvable problem all because I wasn't using the right formula. I was even trying to solve a panic attack through my own powers, which had obviously failed me.

I finally surrendered and made my way to Mom's bedroom. She was sitting on the side of her bed and I fell down next to her and told her I couldn't breathe. She took my pulse with her right hand while dialing 911 with her left. I put my head on her chest as she calmly explained my emergency to the operator. I only remember her saying a few yes's and no's before the paramedics came, each word echoing between the cautious breaths she took so I wouldn't worry about her worrying about me.

Two EMTs walked me out to the steps in my mom's apartment building. I sat as they tried to get a pulse. I could hear a machine beeping when they failed to get some kind of reading. Soon after my sister Kathy arrived, I was put on a cold ambulance and hooked up to an oxygen machine. I was still in my dingy t-shirt and shorts. The last image I saw before the doors closed was my mom standing with her purse on her shoulder, keys in her hand, and Kathy standing next to her in the parking lot. An overcast sky hung behind them. There appeared to be no shocks on the ambulance, but the rough ride didn't really upset me; it helped me get my mind off of myself. I had a very long wait once I got to the hospital. Mom sat with me in the waiting room, then I went in a booth and gave someone my information. I had no insurance, so I was basically telling the hospital how to track me down so they could get their money for the ambulance ride, the oxygen, the wait and whatever shot they were going to give me. After that, I sat back down with Mom in the waiting room. We were very quiet. It was very cold. I was shivering vigorously, despite having on the shoes Mom brought for me. She kept asking for blankets and eventually I was given two thin sheets that did little to keep me warm.

Finally a doctor saw me and I spent a good half-hour in a hospital bed. I was given a shot, told I had had a panic attack and that I should see a physician. Mom sat at my side and Kathy stood, trying to tell jokes.

After I calmed down from the shot, Kathy went home, and Mom took me to her apartment. We were very quiet. Mom was upset she couldn't get a hold of Dad to tell him what happened and I had started developing an obsession with my heartbeat. It was very dark when we got back. I was exhausted from trying to breathe and Mom sat in the living room, which was only illuminated by the TV.

I changed into another set of pajamas and threw away the ones that reminded me of the day I'd had. The task of changing clothes that night seemed to take twice as long as it did that morning. I breathed heavily through the entire process and felt dizzy when I bent down.

Mom sat on the side of the bed as I eased into it. She smoothed out my covers. I don't remember her turning on a light, I just remember her defeated silhouette hanging over me, her arms straddling my legs as they propped her up.

"You okay?" she asked.

"I think so," I lied. "Still a little jittery."

"Try to calm down, Devin." Her voice was a pill that made my eyes close.

I opened my eyes several times during the night. I'd left the door to my room open and every time I woke up, I looked through the doorway, making sure Mom was somewhere in the darkness. Mom's weight on my bed the next morning woke me up. I slowly opened my eyes to find her in the same position she'd been in just hours before, only this time I could actually see her worried face.

"You scared me yesterday," she said as calmly as she could so as not to startle me. "They couldn't get your pulse, Devin, your heart was beating so fast ... you were so pale ... your skin was gray. You were close to having a heart attack." Everything she hadn't said the day before was spilling over. Then finally she said, "Don't ever let worry do that to you again. Don't repeat me."

Mom had health problems her whole life and after I was born, they multiplied. When I was a few months old, she had a heart attack while driving with me and my sister Kathy in the car. She started sweating profusely. She drove all the way to her apartment, stopping the car only after she pulled it onto the sidewalk. Dad was in the ambulance with her when she flatlined. CPR and the defibrillator weren't helping to revive her. The paramedics had given up on her, when Dad demanded that they keep trying.

I was eight when I found her huddled in the corner of her and Dad's bedroom, covered in sweat. She had been sweeping the hardwood floors and her grip on the broom handle seemed to be the only thing keeping her up. I screamed, "Mom!" from the doorway and froze. She panted, "Devin ... get ... your Dad." I ran downstairs and got Dad, who told me to go next door and get Aunt Donna, a nurse, and stay at her and Uncle Glenn's house. My cousins and I watched as Mom was carried down the front stairs on a gurney and into the ambulance.

Other heart attacks and hospital stays followed. All were provoked by worrying about how to make ends meet, whether the car would start or how much it would cost to fix the car if it wouldn't start. Mom used to get frustrated with me when I was a little girl. I had an insatiable need to be liked. I cried a lot when I realized that need would never be fulfilled. My unwillingness to accept that reality made me frustrated and angry, which made me cry even more. It also made me embarrassed to be an individual. I would ask Mom to fix my hair a certain way and if I thought it wouldn't meet my peers' approval, I would take it down and ask her to do it again.

The need to please lessened with each move we made. I never knew how long we were going to stay in a particular city. By the time I started ninth grade, I didn't care who liked me anymore. We had moved three times and three states that year, so I became more devoted to building relationships that could conquer long distance, rather than making false friends.

I'm sure Mom was relieved as she witnessed this growth. All of my lobbying for the popular vote probably wore her out. In fact, I know it did because sometimes she'd say, "Devin, please. I am too old to go through this with you."

Mom saw herself in that part of my development. During her childhood, she was comfortable being herself because the people she grew up with in West Virginia embraced it. When she followed her family to Hamilton, Ohio her individuality was frowned upon. She wasn't used to unfriendliness and open jealousy. She allowed her loneliness to influence a smoking habit that would last more than twenty-five years. She said she walked into a local store one day, "bought some funny books, a Fifth Avenue, a Pepsi and a pack of cigarettes."

But once Granddad told people Mom was a musician, she was in demand. She started playing for and directing several choirs. Her gift became a commodity and I think she realized it would be the only way people would even be motivated to speak to her. I guess she figured, if that was what it took, so be it. Even in her last days, she often said, "If I couldn't play, my phone probably wouldn't ring at all."

As long as she was playing, she was liked and people talked to her, even if it was just to arrange for the next accompaniment. Mom was always aware of her gift from God, but for years, she misused that gift to be liked. When she saw me doing the same thing, it scared her.

There's a chasm between humility and self-degradation and she wanted me to learn the difference long before she did. Mom spent her entire life putting her gifts under a bowl. That's why she wanted me to wear my hair the way I wanted, dance as if my life depended on it, write without pretense and sing authentically—to create like there's no one else in the room except God. To do the opposite is to reduce God to a distant relative who embarrasses you.

I never heard what Mom's playing sounded like before she met Dad and got pregnant with me, but I imagine it sounded quite different. Her playing is the one thing that I think she felt gained approval from her mother, my Grandmother. Before Dad, I think she played not only to distract from her loneliness, but also to please Grandma, who wasn't crazy about her to begin with. Grandma always criticized Mom. No matter what Mom did, it was never good enough and Mom broke her back for her parents, calling them and stopping by their house to make sure they were okay or asking if they needed anything, taking Grandma to the hair salon or just hanging out with Granddad in the family room, watching TV. She even prided herself in never smoking a cigarette in their presence. None of that mattered to my grandparents. Mom was not their favorite and nothing she did changed that.

When she played the piano, Grandma beamed with pride. I think Mom played the way Grandma, who also played piano, wanted to. Mom's ability was discovered when she was three years old. Grandma wasted no time in making sure she received lessons so her gift would be disciplined. Mom was always grateful for that. Because of all that pressure Mom felt, I imagine her playing in her early years lacked spirit. Mom admitted her playing was quite regimented and while I don't really remember her saying when that changed, I imagine it was after she found freedom with my dad.

With my Uncle Bill's help, I finished school in my desired time, which was premature. It probably would've been in my best interest to spend another semester in school, but I was too hard-headed to see I still had some growing up to do. It wasn't even like I had a job waiting for me after I graduated. I spent the next ten months substitute teaching and working as a production assistant at a local TV station.

There were no panic attacks during my last semester. I had a near miss once while I was driving somewhere, though. The little fingers on both my hands began to tingle, a symptom I experienced before my first panic attack. I remember pulling into a hotel parking lot, breathing and praying the possibility of another attack would go away. Shortly after I got back home from school, though, I almost had another attack. Agoraphobia followed.

I would force myself to leave the house, but the further I drove from Mom's, the more nervous I became. Many times my fingers would start tingling and I would pull off of the road.

# LIPS

Mom had the most beautiful lips I've ever seen. They were full and uneven; her bottom lip was fuller than her top one. She had a sexy, pouty, inviting mouth. When Mom's lips were wet with gloss, they were downright delicious. Light would reflect off them like a first-quarter moon hanging over a lake.

Those lips were the source of unending comfort for me growing up: from the words that would roll off of them, to the kisses that would shock my whole body into believing everything would be all right.

She used to make fun of my lips, calling them "white people's lips" because they are thin, a trait I inherited from Dad. She'd say she could always tell when I was upset because my "white people's lips disappear."

When I was a teenager, Mom was driving somewhere, and she told me that, when she was growing up, black girls would suck in their lips to make them appear smaller. She kept her eyes on the road as she said this and I turned to her from the passenger's seat, outraged, and asked, "Why would they do something like that?" Mom kept her eyes on the road and shrugged. "I guess they didn't think their lips were pretty."

Years later, as I was watching Mom put on lip gloss, I said, "Mom, your lips are so pretty." This embarrassed her and she quickly finished putting the gloss on before wrinkling her forehead and saying "Thank you!" A few minutes later, she said, "I used to think my lips were ugly."

My mind immediately went back to that conversation we'd had years before, realizing that she was among those "black girls" she said sucked in their lips.

I didn't bring that previous conversation up, because it was obviously a fragile subject and the older Mom got, the more fragile she became. I just said, "Well, I wish I'd gotten a little more of your lips." Mom always made me feel like the most beautiful person on earth, and I felt it was my relentless duty to do the same for her.

Mom spent very little time in the mirror. She hated spending a lot of time looking at herself, even before she started showing signs of aging. I think that's why she never really learned how to apply makeup. That was just another reason to spend those extra five minutes in the mirror Mom was trying to avoid.

Mom would always buy a lot of makeup, as if to say, "I'm gonna make more of an effort to put this stuff on." Then she'd lose the motivation and go right back to her usual: blush and lip gloss, sometimes foundation or eye shadow. The only cosmetics she ever bothered replacing were the lip glosses. She particularly liked a certain brand I'd started using in middle school, and because Mom always respected my privacy, she didn't use my tube; she bought her own. When she found a kind she liked, she used it up. Most times she wouldn't even look in the mirror to apply it.

It used to annoy me when Mom would call my lips "white people's." I felt like she was teasing me, something I felt should only be reserved for people who didn't claim to love me, like mean peers. But I learned to find the humor in it and realized there was pain behind the humor. It was Mom's way of mocking an insecurity she had about her own lips. She was wondering out loud how she could've given birth to a person with "white people's lips."

It wasn't just lips. It was nose, too. She used to talk about how Dad's recessive nose balanced out her dominant nose to create mine, which is somewhere in between.

I thought Mom's nose was just as beautiful as her lips. Her features made her a unique beauty: strong lips and nose, thick eyebrows, big smiling eyes, pointed chin—the chin she said had no bone in it—and non-intrusive jaw.

All her powerful facial features were on a delicate surface. It contradicted the bones that made up the rest of her body, giving her broad shoulders and long arms and legs. The bones that supported her lengthy fingers and massive palms were strong enough to display her mythical physical presence. But it seemed like when she was being formed in Grandma's womb, that strength lost steam by the time it got to her face. There was just enough left for the features.

The skin that covered that face was delicate, too. I didn't realize just how much so until I touched it when she was in the hospital for the last time.

Mom was very comfortable with her body—especially her 42 DDs—and her sexuality, a confidence she said came from my father's compliments.

Growing up, Mom didn't allow me to say "pinky." She'd always say, "It's little finger, Devin. White people have pinkies." She also would refer to herself as the "white sheep of the family."

She'd say, "I'm already black, so I'm the white sheep of my family."

Mom took that which was supposed to make her feel inferior, and turned it back on itself. During her more than seventy years on Earth, she witnessed and was a recipient of discrimination and bigotry. As a little girl, she watched her grandfather step off a sidewalk in Alabama for a white man to pass. She was very angry at him for doing that and told him so. Watching her father's father become a scared little boy in the presence of a white man lit a fury in her and she rebelled against giving in to the kind of inferiority that ran rampant during her generation and the ones before it in America.

Her use of language empowered her, and because of that, I, too, felt empowered and never felt less than because of my gender, ethnicity, or beliefs. Mom taught me to be comfortable in my own skin long before I even gave any thought to what color it was.

# GOODBYE

There's a certain beauty in Mom's death for me. Besides her being free from physical pain, worry and disappointment, her passing also means we never have to say goodbye to each other again.

Saying it while she was alive was pure misery. It was a reminder that I was leaving her all alone again. I felt like such a tease, popping in and out of her life during holiday breaks from college, then doing it again when I moved to Atlanta. I knew it was necessary for me to live my life, but there was such a guilt that I carried: I was living the life Mom never got to, experiencing what I thought was real independence, free from the burden of family, spouse, or child and experiencing that far from the woman who gave birth to me so I could do it all.

There was always a ritual to my leaving. I would set my alarm clock the night before and knowingly turn it off and go back to sleep when it would go off the next morning. Then Mom would say, "Devin, wake up!" I would hurry up, take a bath. You always took a bath at Mom's, never a shower. The way things were set up in her bathroom weren't even conducive to taking a shower. She had bath beads, bubbles, sweet-smelling perfumes that all invited you to fill up the tub and just sit in it until your skin wrinkled.

I would come out of the bathroom and start packing my dirty underwear and pajamas and all the other little things I didn't pack the night before. Sometimes Mom would gather the few pieces of clothing she washed for me the night before. When I got home, I would just inhale those clothes, so full of the love Mom put into washing them. She would put several fabric softener sheets in the dryer and they would leave a beautiful scent in my clothes that would last for what seemed like months!

Then Mom would busy herself with putting food in grocery bags for me: the bagels she knew she wouldn't eat after I left ("How do you eat that hard bread?"), cream cheese, fruit, soda, and any leftovers she knew I would enjoy for days. Everything Mom cooked was homemade: chicken and noodles, beef and potato soup, collard greens, macaroni and cheese, banana bread. One of my fondest memories of her packing food for me was when she'd baked these incredible oatmeal cookies specifically for me to take home. She put them on a beautiful glass plate that she told me to keep, and put rolls of plastic wrap around it to keep them moist. They barely lasted a week once I got home.

She would double-bag and tie a knot at the top of every bag she filled up for me. Then she would line them up on the dining room table. Then came other odds and ends she'd remember as I started taking my luggage to the car: incense, earrings she didn't wear, lotion she didn't use, pictures she thought I should have, whatever she could think of. Gathering those things distracted her and me from crying.

Even when I was away, I would still be nourished by food that she prepared with her—as she would say—"arthritic hands." I would fill my home with incense that she bought and I would wear earrings that at one time hung from her flesh.

I would ration her homemade banana bread, cookies, or chicken and noodles for as long as I could. One piece of banana bread for dessert one night, two oatmeal cookies the next night. A week later, Mom would ask, "Devin, you're not still eating that chicken and noodles, are you?" I'd always say yes and she'd respond, "Devin! It's probably spoiling by now, please smell it first before you eat it!"

She gave me pieces of furniture from her own home when I moved to Atlanta. I only had my bedroom furniture—the same bed and dresser that she'd bought for me during my junior year in college. She felt bad that she couldn't give me more, but she gave me the essentials: five plates, seven bowls because she knew how much I love to eat cereal, one sauce pan, one frying pan, a set of spatulas and wooden spoons, measuring spoons, a few forks, knives, and spoons, the pastry brush that she left sitting in melted butter in a pot on top of her stove, two coffee mugs, a couple glasses for juice, tall glasses, a wine glass, a plastic Ziploc bag full of sugar on which she wrote "SUGAR" in black marker, salt, pepper, towels, sheets, two comforters, and two pillows. She later mailed me a cookware set she ordered. I still cook with, eat off of, sleep on, and dry off with everything she gave me.

They were all going away gifts for every time I went away, a bon voyage party put together in the final moments before my departure to some new phase in my life.

It was never really goodbye if I always had a reason to come back. I was never so much of an adult that I couldn't call Mom and cry about some challenge or hurt I was dealing with. Mom raised me to be independent, to come up with solutions on my own and find some kind of resolution for resolvable problems. But she also made it okay for me to need my Mommy sometimes. If I ever felt the need to suck it up, it was something I imposed on myself; it was never because of something Mom insinuated.

Mom never made me feel guilty about my singleness. She enjoyed hearing about my life over the phone just as much as when I was telling her in person. She would laugh at my impersonations and bizarre jokes, ooh and aah when I'd describe the new shoes I'd bought, then tell me that I deserved to treat myself when she sensed my guilt. She'd tell me I should be a preacher when I'd go on my here's-what's-wrong-with-the-world tangents, even serving as my Amen corner. Our phone conversations always felt like those of a new romance in which neither party wants to be the first to hang up.

My last goodbye felt familiar. The lump in my throat that would appear during the farewells of my college years showed up again. But this one was monstrous because we both knew we wouldn't see each other on Earth again. We sat in silence for a while, trying to attain the unattainable: more time. I finally said, with a thick throat full of muted screams, "I gotta go, Mom." Mom shook her head as if to say "Don't start, Devin!" I kissed her and started bawling. My Uncle Bill and Aunt Supat were there on each side of me. They walked me out of her hospital room. I turned around one last time and said, "See ya later, Mom."

I wasn't there when she took her last breath a week later. I didn't have to be. There's no such thing as final moments when a relationship transcends such earthly limitations.

My moments with Mom didn't die with her body; they just lived on in a new way. When I first bought my condo, I imagined her sleeping on my couch the same way she slept on her own couch: TV remote resting on her stomach, Ritz crackers and peanut butter on a paper towel next to a Sprite with a straw bouncing in the can on the floor. I would often talk to her, saying things like, "Isn't this nice, Mom?" and I'd hear her say, "It sure is!"

There are times when I long for her so greatly, I'll just whimper, "Oh, Mom ..." and the silence reminds me of the reality that she's gone, but she's still enjoying watching me live my life.

# MAYDAY

The day Mom died was one of the most beautiful I'd ever seen. I was three states away from her in Atlanta and didn't find out she'd died until seven hours after the fact.

For whatever reason, no one called my cell phone to tell me. In retrospect, it was probably a good thing because I was at work when she went to heaven. I can't imagine getting that kind of news in the presence of so many people who didn't know me well.

My shift ended at 10:00 A.M. There was a comforting breeze that greeted me outside the building and stayed with me all day. It felt like a thousand soft tissue papers tickling my skin. I rolled all the windows down in my car, turned up my music and let that wind escort me during my ten-minute drive home. My breathing was so relaxed that day, like I was meditating. I smiled with each breath I took. At stoplights, I reveled in the calm of the day, letting it lay across the bridge of my nose and cheeks.

I felt no urgency to call anyone and ask about Mom's condition. I took my time, dropping off my tote bag in my apartment, then walking to the mailbox. Newly-blossomed trees were swaying about, sounding like a faucet being turned on slowly. I couldn't hear anything else, not even the traffic less than fifty feet away. Halfway to the mailbox, I looked up, took a deep breath, and said, "I love you, Mom."

On the way back to my apartment, I shifted the envelopes in my hands for a moment, took a deep breath and grinned, this time at God. He was conducting the breeze, the sun, and the trees to tell me I would be okay.

Everything in my day-to-day environment was on its best behavior, as if they (my car, my moody refrigerator, and unruly window blinds) knew to give me the space I needed to get the news I was about to receive.

I finally picked up my home phone at 11:00 A.M. The stuttering dial tone let me know I had messages. There were two. The first: alerting me that Mom's condition had worsened. The second: telling me she died.

There were no tears immediately. I erased the messages nervously. There was no need to listen to the inevitable again. I just hung up the phone, held it in my hand, and said, "Okay, Okay ... . um ..." paced a little bit and called Dad.

I was standing the whole time in my bedroom, staring at the carpet.

His tone was so jovial when he answered, "Hey!" I cut across him, "Dad, Mom died." He asked "What?" I repeated myself, adding "... earlier this morning, around 4:30 or so. I didn't find out until just now." He said, "I'm on my way."

Dad appeared in what seemed like an instant. His presence made me feel like I had the whole world in my living room, and I did. He and Mom were my world and now, with him standing in my living room as he did many times before, we were all that was left of what he calls the Trinity. He hugged me tightly, then, stunned, collapsed on my couch. I was frantically searching for phone numbers at this point.

"I thought she was getting better ..." Dad said, trying to figure out how he could've missed any sign that Mom wouldn't be with us anymore.

Then began my I-have-to-call tirade. I started calling off names. Neither Dad nor I had cried yet.

I called to tell my supervisor I wouldn't be at work. Then I started calling Mom's childhood friends. When I hung up after talking to her high school sweetheart, I screamed. It was a short, dry howl. Dad said, "It's okay, Devin, get it out."

I don't remember the exact moment we finally cried. It sort of felt like my soul was floating over us, watching me with my head on Dad's chest, him stroking my arm, his tears falling on my forehead.

It was our first duet without Mom being present.

Dad and I sang together a lot when I was growing up, and Mom either always accompanied us on the piano, or she was in the audience. In that moment of realizing she was gone, our duet had no order. Our voices had become homeless vagabonds who'd run out of earthly options.

LaVergne, TN USA
04 September 2009
157002LV00001B/27/P